MINDELE ANNE TREIP

'Descend from Heav'n Urania': Milton's *Paradise Lost* and Raphael's Cycle in the *Stanza della Segnatura*

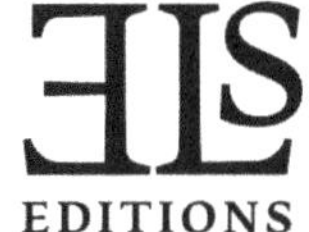

ELS Editions
Department of English
University of Victoria
Victoria, BC
Canada V8W 3W1
www.elseditions.com

Founding Editor: Samuel L. Macey

General Editor: Luke Carson

Printed by CreateSpace

English literary studies monograph series
ISSN 0829-7681 ; 35
ISBN-10 0-920604-23-4
ISBN-13 978-0-920604-23-6

for C.S.T.

CONTENTS

ACKNOWLEDGEMENTS

I have many debts of gratitude to record. Pat Rubin, of the Courtauld Institute, University of London, helped generously with time and Raphael bibliography; we had many stimulating discussions of the Stanza, and she read and advised on the manuscript. Judith Herz has been a tutelary spirit. She, also, found time to read the manuscript; as did Gordon Campbell. Without the close criticisms of these three readers, many more faults would remain. All members of my family contributed in some way. Two of them, A.D.T. and M.S.B., provided taxing and constructive comments on the text. To a third, E.B.T., I have turned constantly for practical and theoretical information in the art history field. I am much indebted, also, to the kind interest of Marvin Spevack in the project. The British School at Rome provided a congenial setting in which to complete this study, and its capable staff assisted me in a multitude of practical details. I am grateful to the Direzione Generale of the Vatican Museums for supplying Raphael photographs from their archives and for giving permission to reproduce them. The emblems from Cesare Ripa, *Iconologie*, edition of J. Baudouin, Paris, 1677, are reproduced by permission of the Syndics of Cambridge University Library.

CHAPTER I

Milton in Rome

Early in 1639, on, possibly, the first of his two lengthy visits to Rome,[1] Milton called on L. Holstenius,[2] at that time librarian to the Barberini, but already working at the Vatican and later principal Vatican librarian, and was received in the Vatican library.[3] In his subsequent graceful letter of thanks, sent to Holstenius at the Vatican address, Milton alludes to some of the literary treasures—the manuscripts and printed texts—which Holstenius had shown him there.[4] But Milton makes no mention in the letter of other artistic treasures he might have seen at the Vatican: for example, the Sistine Chapel, or the Creation cycle (the 'Raphael Bible') in the Loggia; or (known throughout Europe via their numerous sixteenth-century and seventeenth-century engravings) the famous Raphael fresco cycles in the Stanze, the papal suite, especially that in Julius II's personal library, the room since called the 'Stanza della Segnatura'.[5] Nor indeed does Milton anywhere else mention works of art seen in Italy: although we have his poetic and biographical record of some of the literary figures he met and topics he discussed among the distinguished confraternity of humanists, scholars, poets, critics and art patrons (including the eminent Barberini Cardinal who favoured Milton with particular attention) who frequented the academies and private palaces visited by him.[6] Yet Milton, during a total of four months in Rome, must have seen paintings and, one would think, in particular the Vatican Stanze and other frescoes there. Actually to have been at the Vatican and not passed through these famous rooms seems inconceivable. English travellers in the seventeenth century were great viewers; access, even to the Pope's apartments, was possible;[7] the rooms with their frescoes were widely known.[8] As R. Frye observes, Milton's cultivated friends would hardly have allowed him to return home without having seen the principal artistic sights.[9] Having friends like the eminent Manso or introductions such as those to the Barberini or Holstenius, Milton would have had few problems over entrée.

Biographers have from the eighteenth century been puzzled and frustrated by Milton's failure anywhere to include mention of Italian paintings or other artistic sights which he might have seen in his travels.[10] They nonetheless continue increasingly to find general evidences of such impact on *Paradise Lost* especially.[11] J. H. Hanford glimpsed 'analogous expressions' to *Paradise Lost* in the great Italian room cycles or frescoes—thinking more, I suspect, of such simple narrative 'chapters' of Genesis as are illustrated in innumerable Renaissance paintings as well as in the Raphael 'Bible' in the Vatican Loggia; however, Hanford does not name Raphael, alluding instead to Michelangelo and the Sistine Chapel.[12] J. B. Trapp writes along more general lines:[13] Italian art provides a 'background' for *Paradise Lost.*

Frye in his formidable recent volume on *Milton's Imagery and the Visual Arts* continues to exercise caution over even wishing to suggest any direct indebtedness on Milton's part to specific paintings.[14] Although Frye disposes of the old slander about Milton's blindness and thus alleged lack of visual imagination,[15] that ghost may not yet be laid, inasmuch as even in the face of so much stunning visual material strongly recollective of *Paradise Lost* as is included in his book, Frye allows himself to suggest merely that Milton's art reflected "traditional ways of seeing things".[16] Milton's representations of such themes as Adam and Eve, the Fall, the Archangel Michael, the War in Heaven, the rebel angels falling, Satan vanquished in fight, flying angels ('dive-bombing'), the Golden Ladder, the Holy Spirit as Dove, or the Son as Creator, all conform quite closely to traditional motifs common to Renaissance or at least to mediaeval iconography,[17] or follow techniques and styles peculiar to baroque or illusionist paintings of the later Renaissance.[18]

In pursuing such analogies, Frye does not cite Raphael in any major contexts. He finds a few on the whole general parallels in *Paradise Lost* to two paintings of Raphael ('St. Michael', and the Loggia 'Creation of the Animals') and parallel minor details to one or two others, 'The Disputà' also being cited.[19] However, on one detail Frye is explicit about a direct influence or recollection of Raphael in *Paradise Lost.* That is Milton's unusual depiction of the birth of the animals out of the ground in *Paradise Lost,* Book VI. This, Frye thinks, could only have been remembered from the 'Creation of the Animals' in the Loggia, where God the Father is seen similarly calling the animals up out of the ground, as if the earth is in parturition: an unusual feature.[20] Here, Frye concedes, may be proof positive of Milton's direct indebtedness to Raphael. Except for the passing detail of the globe of angels from the 'Disputà', Frye does not mention Raphael's famous cycle in the Stanza della Segnatura. An iconographer perhaps, Frye does not write as an iconologist (to make use of Gombrich's distinction[21]): Frye is not concerned with interpretative analysis, although many of the pictures he deals with are highly charged with figurative meaning or allegory. It is possible therefore that Frye's concern with pictorial details may obscure larger conceptual themes and designs in Raphael's or other allegorical cycles which may stand in significant correspondence with parallel themes and structures in *Paradise Lost.* It has sometimes been felt that Michelangelo could have influenced Milton. But of all Italian Renaissance painters, it might surely have been Raphael, the most intellectual and the most 'gracious', with his great Creation cycles in the Vatican Loggia and his Stanze or other paintings famous for their complex erudite *imagini*, great allegorical conceits unifying ceilings and walls, indeed entire rooms, as in the 'Segnatura' or the Chigi Chapel—*imagini* subsuming figures and themes from Scripture and myth, philosophy, knowledge, religion and theology, conjoining Old and New Testament motifs with classical—it might surely have been the learned and harmonious Raphael whose work would have struck the deepest response in Milton as a humanist and religious poet.

The notion that a ceiling, or a wall fresco, or a whole room may illustrate and develop a coherent intellectual idea may appear unfamiliar at first to students of literature, although it will be instantly recognizable to students of literary allegorical narrative. However, such a view seems to have been a commonplace in sixteenth-century painting and painting theory and art criticism from the fifteenth century onwards.[22] It is known that by the mid-sixteenth century (but starting much earlier) there had developed sophisticated and complex programmes, painters' libretti, so to speak, sometimes constructed by humanist advisers for particular decorative projects, often on mythological and allegorical subjects commissioned by the patron, who might be imagined, rather as with a masque, as prescribing the theme in general, rather than himself providing all the details, which would more probably be worked out either by the adviser or perhaps, in other cases, by the artist in consultation with one or more such persons.[23] Such programmes, whoever constructed them, whether *ante hoc* or *ad hoc*, or however rigorously (or otherwise) followed by the artist, would necessarily have their iconographic roots in "the canonic texts of religion and antiquity,"[24] and of course in later visual symbolism embodying those. Their designs might at the same time be rooted in older decorative conventions, such as the mediaeval 'Liberal Arts' cycle, itself partly allegorical: in this, a personified Virtue or similar figure is seen presiding above human exemplars depicted below. A scheme of the latter kind, or a synthesis of several such, evidently was an important starting point for Raphael's decoration of the Stanza della Segnatura.[25] An extraordinary late example of such a fully worked out programme is A. Caro's minutely particular exposition, addressed to T. Zuccaro, of how to develop in a painting the "soggetto... di cose appropriati alla solitudine".[26] The "soggetto" or theme is broken down, or conversely we might say is amplified, into parts and aspects, greater or lesser, abstruse or practical, religious and secular, all exactly fitted into the vault's physical design and co-ordinated with the shapes, sizes and distribution of the sub-compartments of the ceiling space: so that intellectual relationships within the larger theme may be seen developing visually. This is analogous to the manner in which an orator might amplify his *inventio* and he or a poet work out his *dispositio*. Or, for that matter, to the way in which a literary allegorist such as Spenser develops and breaks down his general theme of virtue in the forming ('gentle discipline') into the various virtues (knights), their adventures, sub-parts and sub-adventures with their sub-protagonists, all deployed in such a way as to show the underlying relation with the main theme. And why should a painter also not be free to develop his 'idea' in such a manner? For if poetry may resemble painting, then surely paintings may also be like poetry.[27]

A vivid example of such a programme fully executed, or the harmonious development of a single theme (the harmony of the spheres) across a unified space, exists in the mosaic dome of the Chigi Chapel, executed to Raphael's design. On a simple level, we can see that he has used the lower parts of the dome, divided into eight main sections, to illustrate the eight (in this case) moving or starry spheres, each with its attendant angel and astrological sign, while God the Father is framed in the cupola, apparently above the main dome—and so evidently above the spheres. Drastic foreshortening makes it appear as if we are standing virtually underneath him, while he is looking down into the spheres through the opening of the cupola, which is not only a dramatic frame but, because of the attendant *putti* clustering around the edge and peering down, also reminds us that God is beyond the universe. One might guess then that the solid rim of the cupola itself represents the outermost or fixed sphere; and that God is standing upon the outside of that ultimate enclosure.[28] The effect is accentuated by the *putti* of whom only heads and hands can be seen looking over the edge—as if they were taking particular care not to fall out through the hole and from so great a height. The composition does more than merely illustrate in a static way God the Father presiding from above the *primum mobile* over his cosmic creation below. We observe that the angels do not merely occupy their spheres; each seems to be energetically pushing or driving his own sphere around (the concentric spheres have to be presented as if seen in a flat plane, or rather running around the dome, a part circle seen in each instance). Their energy is matched by God's dramatic gesture, arms flung up and back—whether this is a 'creating' action, or an energizing gesture, or one reflecting the divine *meraviglia* at the Creation, or some other (a 'receiving' or 'calling up' action, as J. Shearman suggests[29]), we cannot be sure. We also observe that whereas some angels look up rather anxiously toward Heaven, others are looking down. As we begin to reflect on these details and their possible significance, we can surmise that more recondite meanings lie behind the whole composition, over and beyond the familiar conception of the celestial spheres.[30]

It seems likely that Raphael would have had the assistance of some such learned mentor or mentors as were represented in the programme of A. Caro, in helping him to construct the even more complex cycle in the Stanza della Segnatura: possibly one or more of a group of humanist scholars such as those later gathered in the Farnese circle of A. Caro, P. Giovio, Vasari and others.[31] Exactly who might have helped Raphael, or to what degree he himself amplified his 'inventions' (his 'sopraumane idee', as Bellori expressed it[32]) evidently is not known;[33] but the length and detail of Vasari's early descriptions of the room and of all later critical expositions from Bellori onward suggest that it was commonly assumed that a complex and to some degree individually amplified meaning or meanings must underlie the compositions. The fact that the ceiling may have been completed last, and as a kind of 'summing up' of the full message of the room after that had evolved,[34] renders both suppositions (a complex and composite programme; and Raphael's participation in adapting it) more likely. It is evident that with the Stanza one has progressed far behond the conventional 'Liberal Arts cycle'—although such a scheme has evidently been Raphael's starting point. With the Stanza, the issue of mere illustration has turned to one of 'expansion'[35] of a particular theme, of a much more sophisticated sort, into which many different kinds of allusions or subordinate programmes may be incorporated within a larger programme or scheme unified but intricate, and to which each subsequent interpreter, like the artist himself, can bring something further.[36] We have not now mere pictorial representation accompanying flat allegorical personifications but, in Gombrich's words, 'symbolic images' woven into a meaningful design: not 'pittura' or 'storia' but, to use the favoured word of the earlier period, *imagini*:[37] allegorical images.

It is against this tradition that I want to discuss first Raphael's Stanza and particularly his 'Astrology', earlier so called: a rather complex and semi-divine 'Urania' figure, as I shall argue, with a variety of cosmic, Creation, providential and still further associations. This figure speaks to us not as 'simple narrative' but as such an *imagine*, coming to Raphael probably already charged with complex associations. I then shall try to relate to the dominant 'conceit' of the Stanza and to Raphael's presiding figures and especially his 'Astrology' or 'Urania' (if rightly *she* is called), Milton's figure of the same name and equally ambivalent identity. My hope is that by so doing we shall elucidate not only Milton's Muse (her 'meaning', not just her 'name') but, much more widely, Milton's themes and intentions in his four Invocations, and the larger relationship of the latter to his poem: the 'programme' according to which the Invocations reveal themselves and declare their mutual interrelations and their correlations with the poem's main narrative sections. To understand the way in which the unified conceit of Raphael's room works is, to some extent, I shall argue, to understand the way in which Milton's own mind and scheme are working.

CHAPTER II

The Stanza della Segnatura: Vault and 'Urania'

It would seem that commentary on Raphael's Stanza illustrates two conflicting impulses which have persisted in the history of art criticism, as of literary criticism. There is the one school which resists the 'imposition' (so-called) of allegorical constructs upon the original text in favour of narrative or structural or other formal analysis: and the other which (to refer again to Gombrich) aims at "the reconstruction" of a pre-existing "programme"[1] (in Renaissance literary terms, the antecedent 'Idea'[2]) around which the artifact supposedly is built. Vasari's notably early account of the Stanza in the *Lives* is basically of the first order:[3] proceeding picture by picture and detail by detail, endeavouring to uncover in the manner of an historian or antiquarian the mythological meanings (for him as for Cartari largely secular) signified by the details of the costumes of the four main *tondi* figures, in the corner rectangles (that is, the panels in the spandrels) the subjects of the scenes, and on the walls the identities of the historical figures and the names of their books.[4] Yet from 1550 if not earlier the feeling, amounting at times to conviction, has persisted that there was a unified (if numinous) meaning to the entire room far beyond the merely exemplificatory, and profundities not explained even by the fact that the cycle may have had roots in more than one genre of 'programme'.[5] Especially it has been felt that the vault itself holds a particular significance, or indeed the key to the entire room.

Any eye may discern that there are two significant directions of movement (in design, as well as in terms of intellectual content) on the vault or emanating from it. The first movement joins together the four ladies of the *tondi* (Poetry, Theology, Justice and Philosophy) in their matching globes or circles surrounding the central heavenly octagon,[6] as the eye travels around the ceiling in an endless circle, and in addition (via the intervening rectangles) links each adjacent or nearly contiguous pair of ladies more specifically with each other. And the second direction of movement, instead of revolving round the ceiling and its heavenly centre, runs from the ceiling *downward* to the walls below (the frescoes known as 'The Parnassus', 'The Disputà', a more fragmented wall concerned with Justice, and 'The School of Athens'). The downward movement is conveyed by the striking positioning of each presiding figure directly above that painting with a correspondent subject on the wall immediately below her, and by other more specific connecting details. (I shall discuss three of these ceiling figures and two of the wall paintings more fully later.) It is mainly I think the second of these two arresting and complementary movements which has led Gombrich (partly following earlier critics) to assert that there is in the scheme of the room as a whole (which loses its meaning if fragmented) not only a statement of the "essential unity of all human disciplines"[7] (the theme of Knowledge and the Liberal Arts being appropriate to a room intended for a library), but more profoundly an expression of the idea that "the whole universe [is] a hierarchy of principles emanating and descending from all [*sic*] high" (from the vault, that is, down to the walls). The walls then display those principles as human "embodiments ... however incomplete, of [the same] general ideas or principles"—they are "expositions or amplifications of the ideas expressed by the personifications on the ceiling". Exactly what becomes manifest from on high in the Stanza is indicated more precisely by the inscriptions which accompany each of the four principal ladies in the *tondi*: according to Gombrich, it can all be summed up as "knowledge and virtue as expressions of the divine".[8] The unified room, vault and walls, and as much by the linking of the figures on the vault with each other as by their connections downwards with their walls, thus tells us as plainly as may be that the source of all forms of knowledge or wisdom is in God alone, and comes down as a gift from the divine source to men in their various intellectual pursuits on Earth.

It seems that in a number of important aspects Gombrich has developed the reading of the Stanza by G. Bellori in 1695. The conceits on Raphael's vault derive, says Bellori

> da un solo principio, e da un solo argomento, qualmente si disse avanti. Ilche sarà manifesto, se ci solleviamo coll'intelletto, considerando che la Teologia, la Filosofia, la Giurisprudenza, ò vero la Giustizia con la Poesia sono quattro parti principali della Sapienza, da cui dipende la norma della virtù, e l'umana felicità nella vita attiva, e contemplativa. L'huomo dunque come di mente partecipe ricorre alla divina mente, quasi rivo à fonte.... A queste trè imagini fù aggiunta la quarta del Monte Parnaso, e della Poesia per le ragioni di sopra addotte dell'antichità sua, e della sapienza de' Poeti, da cui l'altre scienze, come da fonte, sono derivate.[9]

Bellori stresses more explicitly perhaps even than Gombrich how it is that we are to understand that all forms of wisdom (all four ladies) are parts of the divine. An earlier passage is also relevant: the four walls, the four ladies above in the *tondi*, as well as the smaller quadrants in the spandrels, all contribute to the "gran concetto" and derive from "un solo principio", which is "la Sapienza delle cose divine, ed umani".[10] Thus the whole room expresses both the unity of all forms of knowledge in the divine mind and also the dependence of human upon divine wisdom. Bellori does not articulate very well that descent or downward movement which Gombrich finds so essential to the Stanza and so brilliantly expounds; nevertheless, the notion of divine descent to the human or at least unbroken interconnectedness is strongly felt by him in all its numinousness.

It seems likely that even Vasari reflected something of the prevalent earlier feeling that there was a mysterious synthesis in the Stanza—if only in his repeated stress on the positional relationship of each "allegorical" Lady (he uses that term) to her respective wall (that is, divine above human in each subject); also *next* to a related subject in at least one of her two adjacent rectangles.[11] Certainly his opening statement is itself suggestive of synthesis: "cominciò nella camera della Segnatura una storia quando i teologi accordano la filosofia e l'astrologia con la teologia . . .".[12] More recent critics have found in the Stanza or various parts of it comparable if not so comprehensive 'reconciliations' as Bellori or Gombrich discerned. E. Wind, for example, evolving a useful term, speaks of various 'concordances' in the room and particularly of that expressed through the presiding figure of Justice.[13]

With these general remarks on the critical background, designed to reinforce the point that Raphael's room must be interpreted as a whole, I wish now to examine more particularly those elements in the Stanza which most concern *Paradise Lost.* According to Gombrich's directive and the feeling of earlier critics, I shall 'read' the room from the vault (or rather its apex) downward.[14]

Remembering that the ceiling is *vaulted*, the highest part is at the roundel which (like the cupola of the Chigi Chapel) displays *divini amori* looking down over or standing at the very edge of the octagonal space, empty save for clouds: the Papal arms float *forward* of and not *in* Heaven (since one of the two *putti* who support it is distinctly seen standing just forward of the edge of the roundel). Thus the octagon for all practical and non-denominational purposes is Heaven, and in its brightness resides God (invisible in light).

Revolving around him, as it were (since one has to turn each time to see the next figure) are the four representations in the heavenly globes on the next lower level of the vault. Reading to the right, as one enters the room at the corner under 'Astrology' (the figure whom I hope later to define as a semi-divine 'Urania'), these are: Poetry, Theology, Justice and Philosophy (who brings us back round to face the door). The details of their dress (described minutely by Vasari[15]) plus the inscriptions on the tablets accompanying them indicate their general characters and also more precisely what they stand for. It is not difficult to perceive that these imposing beings are more than just representatives of four branches of knowledge or liberal arts (which they do also epitomize). Their equal positions high on the ceiling; the clouds under their feet; the enthroned seats; the divine winged *amori* flanking each figure and (as next to the Gospels in 'The Disputà') holding up tablets with inscriptions; all indicate that these four ladies are very special beings, heavenly or celestial in nature. They are also, conspicuously, sister figures, parallel in all respects save for their specialized costumes and one or two other significantly differing details; linked closely not only by their equal celestial globes but almost physically by the decorative double bosses, which connect the globes with each other (via the rectangles one step lower) and also directly with the central octagon (so to speak with Heaven). (The small pairs of intervening paintings, Sodoma's, also form visual connectors.) Poetry alone among the four is winged. The question of why these four particular figures are associated and why Poetry is included is largely resolved by the inscriptions on their respective tablets.[16] All are forms of *knowledge*, or rather of divine *wisdom* in the first instance. Two figures might be said to represent *inspired* knowledge (poetic-prophetic; or directly revealed): Poetry[17] ("numine afflatur", 'the divine rapture') and Theology ("divinar[um] rer[um] notitia", 'knowledge of things divine'). The other two figures perhaps represent those forms of knowledge which are regulated in the divine mind, as in men's, according to definable *laws*: Justice ("ius suum unicuique tribuit", 'to each his due'—in the painting on the wall below are representations of the civil and the canon law) and Philosophy ("causarum cognitio", 'knowledge of causes', which I take to be *first* causes: since lesser human philosophy, moral and natural, are illustrated on the wall below). The design of the vault says clearly then that all these four revolve around or emanate from one and the same divine source.

Simultaneously, the room design says as well that these four ladies also connect Heaven with earth: inasmuch as each not only presides over the *amplificatio* on the wall below her, but three of the ladies also point to or gesture downward with an approximate orientation toward the centres of their respective pictures. The line of Poetry's arm leads us to the 'Parnassus', on the hill of which is shown Apollo playing to the nine Muses, with accompanying figures of great poets of the past, Homer and Dante for example, grouped nearby, poets pagan and Christian, past and recent. Theology points directly to the so-called 'Disputà',[18] which shows God the Father, Christ and the Holy Spirit in fact *instructing* or *illuminating* the Scriptures for the benefit of patriarchs, saints and sages, past and present; and Philosophy gestures down toward 'The School of Athens', which *does* show a concourse of sages and philosophers, including probably Socrates and Plato, discussing or disputing. Justice does not point down, rather brandishes her sword upward.[19] (She is set above the triptych showing the other three Cardinal Virtues, this in turn surmounting the window which is flanked by scenes of the Canon and Civil Law.) Justice however *looks* down: whereas the other three ladies gaze into unknown distances—all with clearly differentiated and extraordinarily meaningful expressions. Such details make the ladies of the celestial globes themselves individual *amplificationes* of the divine wisdom, or of these four particular aspects of it. Thus the four ladies embody the double truth, that all forms of wisdom emanate equally from and coexist in the divine source and are thereby related *intra se* ('sisters'); and that (as Gombrich says) all human knowledges, or truth (I would substitute 'truth' for 'virtue'), flow down from on high.

So much for the *tondi*. But there is a still further intermediate or 'mediating' level between ceiling and walls, heaven and earth. In the lower parts of the vault, that is, immediately above each angle of the room, there are painted onto the convexes of the four spandrels four rectangular panels containing scenes dominated by certain figures. These depict, going around the ceiling in the same order as before, the flaying of Marsyas by Apollo (between Poetry and Theology); the temptation of Adam by Eve at the Tree (between Theology and Justice); the Judgement of Solomon (between Justice and Philosophy); and 'Astrology', as Vasari calls her (although that name comes to seem increasingly inadequate to her perceived role), above a transparent representation of the universe, or the celestial spheres. This figure (who has no attached name in the painting, and whom I shall refer to as 'Urania') is well described by Bellori as "soprastando avanti" (standing above and forward):[20] that is, her position on the spandrel puts her somewhat below and forward of the four principal ladies, as she leans forward over her transparent globe (which is evidently an orrery). She, like her companion figures in the other rectangles, is by virtue of her actual physical position that degree closer to earth. Although the relevances of Apollo-Marsyas and 'Astrology'-'Urania' are not entirely obvious, it can be seen that even in the simplest terms the subject of each rectangle relates to both the adjacent ladies in the two *tondi* alongside—so indicating the intellectual interconnectedness of these pairs.[21] For example, it is obvious that Solomon embodies Justice (the legal judgement) on the one hand, and Wisdom on the other (a 'fairness' which transcends mere crude equality). And on his one hand are in fact Justice and on the other Wisdom. Also we can see that Adam and Eve relate both to Old Testament Justice (God's punishment of the Fall) and to Christian theology (Original Sin leads to the Redemption). But the extraordinary, lyrical, barbaric scene of Apollo playing oblivious (rapt in the literal sense), while a triumphant attendant (back to us) with the one hand crowns Apollo, looking at him, while with the other arm and his body he merges with the pair of figures who are flaying Marsyas (tied to a tree), presents us with a conundrum. The song contest which Marsyas so unfortunately for himself lost and Apollo with his lyre won obviously relates to Poetry: but the affinity of such a subject as this with Theology is obscure and disturbing. Similarly, the 'Astrology', in her connection with astronomy or more accurately with the supra-terrestrial spheres, may concern one aspect of Philosophy: but her relation to Poetry or certainly divine poetry is less apparent.

However, in interpreting the rectangles we shall do better to adopt the allegorical and typological modes of reading habitual to an earlier Christian humanist tradition, rather than our own secular and rather literal habits. Pictures of the complex kind under discussion (and perhaps especially in a sacred place) are not likely to be simple illustrations of mythological scenes or simple representations of personified abstractions; they do not necessarily 'say' merely what they record on their narrative surfaces. We note that we have in the ceiling rectangles two pairs of subjects: two Old Testament and two classical. This in itself is suggestive. For the Renaissance used both Old Testament and pagan motifs not merely in loose association but specifically as adumbrations: the one more strictly as 'types' (prototypes) of central Christian doctrines or Christological themes; the other sometimes as 'types' and sometimes more loosely, as allegorized renderings of moral or spiritual meanings drawn out of the pagan myths. So read, the rectangles offer more coherence in their settings. Thus Solomon *anticipates* both the Justice of God and (perhaps) the infinite Wisdom or Mercy of God and Christ;

and Adam and Eve not only represent the Fall of Man with his punishment in the Expulsion but also *prefigure* (in Christian terms) the doctrine of Original Sin, which in its happier aspect is the *felix culpa*: so inferring the Redemption through Adam's seed. And already we begin to see, through these linking rectangles, that the roles of Theology, Justice and Philosophy overlap, are indeed 'reconciled'. We also realize that we can read the ceiling rectangles both to the *right*, and to the *left*: they make sense either way. And it becomes evident that according to which direction and at what level we read them, we shall find somewhat differing emphases and pick out supporting details. Thus, reading right from the Fall panel, the rather strange expression on Eve's face—knowing, half-sinister, yet also delphic (her eyes look beyond Adam)—and the central stress on the tree and fruit (the tiny, fatal apple held in her forefinger and thumb, dead centre of the picture) indicate to us that the focus at this moment is on *knowledge*: secular knowledge with all its allurements. In this context we become aware that human *scientia* (the apple and tree) may anticipate but is far inferior to *divinarum rerum notitia.*

Similarly, the classical figures, allegorized and Christianized, also conform to 'types' or looser 'pagan vestiges' of Christianity. The seemingly savage scene of Marsyas can be seen as not only prefiguring the displacement of pagan poetry by divine (Christian) poetry (adjacent in the *tondo*)—just as Apollo's lyre itself could be seen to symbolize the displacement of a more primitive era of poetry by a more sophisticated (Greek lyre in place of panpipes)—but, on the other side (Theology), in a more spiritual allegory as a kind of Christian triumph of spirit over body.[22] Marsyas is, after all, all but crucified on that tree; although his arms do not form the shape of the cross,[23] he is crucified, his side is cut (high on the right of his chest, in the same place as is displayed Christ's wound in 'The Disputà'), and his demeanour is strangely passive. But Apollo's transport, his crown of glory and his right index finger evidently pointing up to Heaven show him as oblivious to the torment of poor Marsyas, which is registered sympathetically on the face of the attendant who is flaying. Some form of Christianized interpretation seems unavoidable in the painting, in my view, and renders the triumphant yet spiritual expression on the face (seen side-view) of the central figure and Apollo's own absorbed abstraction more comprehensible.

The Marsyas-Apollo panel in fact offers a very complex allegorical case. All commentators on the Ovid (the story originates in *Metamorphoses*, VI) call attention to the cry of the flayed satyr: "quid me mihi detrahis?" (line 385). "Why do you take me out of myself?" For poetic inspiration does draw the poet out of himself; in the words of one of Milton's epic predecessors, it makes "le poète se surmont[er] soi-mesme".[24] Edgar Wind's interpretation of the Marsyas story is perhaps unduly emotive: "The torture of the mortal by the god who inspires him".[25] Yet there is undoubtedly something about Raphael's interpretation of the story that makes of his composition something quite different from Ovid, and also something more compelling than an allegory of poetic inspiration. In Raphael's picture, Apollo and Marsyas are visually joined, via the intervening figures of the two attendants. The arm of the one with the knife rests on Marsyas' side, the outstretched arm of the other with the crown brushes Apollo's head; while the arms and legs of the attendants themselves seem to melt together in the centre of the picture. Thus the unbroken line connecting all four figures appears to suggest that the god's triumph arises directly out of the satyr's agony: bodily-spiritual anguish, passing into inspiration-rapture-glory. Looking also at the way the Raphael panel is set into interaction with the adjacent *tondi* figures of divine Poetry and Theology, we might conclude that there may be a strongly typological (though not necessarily Christological) bearing. For example, one might think that the scene illustrates well the text from Eph. 4. 22-24: "Put off your old nature [old man] and put on your new nature [new man]". Or, equally appropriately, in view of the emphasis on music in the Marsyas panel, the text, "Sing to the Lord a new song", from Psalm 33.3 or Is. 42.10: in which case Apollo's triumph in the song-contest with the satyr could signify a new, redeemed genre of Christian poetic inspiration. That would have been a very congenial concept to Milton. The choice depends, again, on which direction we read: toward Theology, or toward Poetry. Or perhaps all these meanings are subsumed.

'Urania' offers an even more complex case, which I shall want to discuss separately. But we can see, speaking briefly, that as 'she herself who fixes the . . . stars in their places', she is something more divine than the mere human study of astronomy. She can on the one hand lead us to the 'understanding of [prior] causes', or divine Philosophy; while on the other, she relates either to Poetry's lyre, in her own music of the spheres, and/or to Poetry's wings—the winged flights of imagination—'Urania' too being placed 'so high above the spheres'.[26] As will later be noted, 'Urania' (so named) also had in the Renaissance a long-standing connection with serious poetry. It is to be observed, significantly, that both the higher 'Urania' and the Apollo of the rectangles are much more dramatic and important figures, much more clearly charged with symbolic import, than are the Apollo and Urania figures on the 'Parnassus' wall below them. The lower, more human figures both raise eyes heavenwards, indicating rapture or inspiration, but their recumbent positions are not dynamic.[27]

Thus we see that the whole ceiling sequence may be read uninterruptedly either to the right, or to the left.[28] All eight figures flow harmoniously into each other: and all the four *tondi* figures acquire a degree of co-identity as between themselves, via their shared rectangles. If we read *left* from each *tondo*, Poetry becomes connected with Theology via the double, poetic and quasi-religious, aspects of Apollo; Theology with Justice via the New as distinguished from the Old Testament interpretation of Adam's sin; Justice with Philosophy via Solomon's just and wise judgement; and Philosophy with Poetry via 'Urania' as both cosmic order and also music or poetry. Or, if we read in the reverse direction, from the *right* of each *tondo*, we arrive backwards at the same connections. It does not matter which way we look or read; all four rectangles, and all four *tondi* figures, flow uninterruptedly into each other, resolving mysteriously into one, revolving endlessly in an unbroken circle around their heavenly source. Contraries and reconciliations; paradoxes and resolutions; differences and co-identities; classical and scriptural; Old and New Testament: all these meanings merge in a sublime and quite dazzling visual and intellectual unity.[29] Not only are the separate aspects of the divine mind shown as essentially one: but mediation between divine and human wisdoms, between heaven and earth, is shown as continually taking place—both in pre-history, through those great human 'types' or adumbrations of the Old Testament and Greek myth, and also more directly via the celestial *mediatrice* who continually bring the divine inspirations and wisdoms of Poetry, Theology, Justice and Philosophy down to earth and into men's present lives.

Of the corner rectangles, that showing 'Urania', even more than Apollo-Marsyas, is especially compelling: the close association of Poetry-Urania-Philosophy having long been sensed as being of special importance, deep but not obvious. Although she shares their mediating function, there are some singularities about 'Urania' which set her apart from her companion figures of the other three rectangles. For one thing, she seems closer in a number of features to the other four ladies of the *tondi*. Although not enthroned, she is the only other personified female figure on the ceiling, in this matching the *tondi* figures. She too is flanked by winged *divini amori*, indicating that she has something of a semi-divine status; and hers is the only rectangle figure not depicted as upon the earth. To make use of Milton's words, where all the others are 'standing on earth', she only is 'rapt above the Pole'. Although 'Urania's' feet do not rest on clouds like those of the ladies of the *tondi*, the feet of her attendant *putti* conspicuously do. She belongs in the heavens, it would seem; but (with her lower body half seen through the transparent model of the universe) she seems to be set more nearly down toward the level of the created cosmos. While still 'above the spheres' she is, one might imagine, in her loving scrutiny seen as if longing to descend down into the cosmos. More factually, whereas the *amori* of the four *tondi* hold their tablets high up for us to read plainly the inscriptions, those holding 'Urania's' tablets seem to be drawing away from her and holding the tablets *away* from her or us: their faces turn toward her but their bodies turn away. I say 'tablets', because the fact that all the other *putti* of the *tondi* are holding tablets makes us at first suppose that these are what 'Urania's' *putti* also hold; but a closer view makes us see, from their slightly different shape and from the way they are held under the arms of the *putti*, that these 'tablets' must almost certainly be *books*. At any rate, those tablets, or books, would appear to be *blank*.[30] It is as if they are withholding her identity, whereas all the other pairs of *amori* proclaim. Is there a deliberate reluctance on Raphael's part to name or delimit this figure too closely? We know from her physical position between them that this 'Urania' figure has connections with both divine Poetry and divine Philosophy: but it would appear that she is less a mythic adumbration of those (like the other rectangle figures) than something in herself unique and of divine potency. Vasari in his matter of fact way rather avoids the problem, referring to the rectangle briefly as that belonging to 'Astrology', and where "è ella medesima che pone le stelle fisse e l'erranti a' luoghi loro".[31] Bellori avoids any name, referring to her as "una donna", and eventually arrives at a rather wider interpretation in which Contemplation seems to be clearly included.[32] Later art historians down to the present have shared the disinclination to interpret 'Urania' too narrowly and have elaborated still further on Bellori. Thus there has indeed been difficulty over the name as well as the meaning of 'Urania', not only in Milton's mind.[33]

The other details of the 'Urania' figure's appearance are equally absorbing. Her costume, like that of her four half-sisters (if I may so call them) is highly symbolic. The wispy veil which Raphael has so cleverly drawn twisted round and round her as if windswept, and fastened at the top of her head like a tiara, on another view may itself seem to resemble the planetary wheelings of the spheres over which 'Urania' presides. In colour, it can be seen like the orrery or globe itself to be sprinkled with stars (not so, I think, her dress). And the pin which holds the scarf in place at her waist appears to be itself a miniature orrery. There is also, dimly visible across 'Urania's' star-sprinked globe, a spectrum showing shadowy figures of the zodiac. Such details clearly illustrate 'Urania's' traditional cosmic aspect: which yet appears to be but one aspect of her rôle here. She is placed, as I have said, *above* the eight (or nine) spheres, which must put her at the level of the *primum mobile*, the realm immediately below God. One of her hands rests on the outermost sphere of what Milton calls the World (not the solar universe merely, which is a small part of the whole). The hand supports her there quite firmly, as if resting on a solid surface. Yet wonderfully she, and we, can also see through the sphery globe: as if it were transparent (or glassy). Her other hand is flung upward, as if in a gesture of spontaneous admiration or wonder. This is confirmed by the intent and rapt expression on her face (which has just a trace of a smile) as she bends down over the globe, her body straining slightly as if to see more clearly down into the starry depths. Her face and gesture can only be described (and often have been) as of a heavenly beauty and graciousness. But *wonder*, *meraviglia*, at the created cosmos so visibly spread out below her, is the overriding impression communicated by this entire figure: and no better description of this can be found than Bellori's own words: "Ella soprastando avanti, vi posa sopra una mano, e d'inalza l'altra per meraviglia della grand' opera del fabbro eterno".[34] As Bellori so well catches in the spirit of the painting, this 'Urania' is far from being only the human science of Astronomy. She is the spirit of *wonder* at the great work of God in the created universe, seen as if for the first time in its pristine splendour: the Book of Nature, traditionally the subject of contemplation by God's creatures. And by God: ever since God first looked at his work and saw that it was good. For we may observe that in the painting the view which 'Urania' perceives is not the view of the heavens as we should see them, looking *up*: but the view as God or the angels would see them, looking *down* and *into* the spheres. It corresponds with the view God has looking down from the cupola of the Chigi Chapel. We see 'Urania' a little as we see God in the chapel, that is from below (and curiously, also partly from above). She is distant: yet much closer than the remote Father of the chapel. Thus, the 'activity' of 'Urania' (who might be thought to be doing nothing) is conspicuously that of Contemplating. It is the *vita passiva*, as opposed to the *vita attiva*. Perhaps as Bellori hinted, she is the Divine Contemplation itself—one of the forms of God's wisdom—hence her position contiguous with 'Understanding of [first] Causes'. In this respect she is a higher manifestation of the related activity in human beings—'contemplation of created things'—which (in Milton's words) does or should lead men back to God. In fact, she could be read as the Divine Mind contemplating its own handiwork in the Creation.[35] The 'Urania' panel in this light becomes typologically predicative, becomes a Creation scene. Classical image ('Astrology'-Urania), then, symmetrically balances the Old Testament image in the diagonally correspondent panel on the opposite side of the vault.

'Urania's' connections with Poetry are less conspicuous but nevertheless clearly present. We do not even have to look to the music of the spheres. Her rapture links her with Apollo's inspired attitude and expression in the corresponding rectangle: god and goddess are seen as equally 'rapt'—oblivious in their private transport—hence, appropriately, flanking the goddess who embodies the 'numine afflatur'. We shall remember that there is also a Urania figure on the Parnassian hill below: poets have always sung of the heavens. 'Urania' enraptured must also put us in mind of the long tradition, extant already in Raphael's time but whether in painting or in poetry first is hard to determine, which turns the cosmic muse Urania (perhaps because she *is* 'celestial') specifically into the patroness of divine poetry and especially that tradition of long poetic narrative dealing with Creation matter and the Christian epic.

Raphael's 'Urania' therefore might be thought to mean so much as to be, appropriately, not nameable. Her composite significance is in keeping with her own distinctive situation above the spheres, her appearance and pose and her resemblances to her 'sister' ladies: as also with her position flanking the figures of Poetry and Philosophy. The special synthesis which she effects in that important corner of the Stanza vault is thus by way of becoming yet another subordinate 'programme' merged into the principal design. 'Urania' is that divine science which created, ordered and still presides over 'the visible diurnal sphere' (in men, mirrored in their study of its workings); she reflects divine and human *meraviglia* at the wonders of the created cosmos, thereby also embodying the theme of divine and human Contemplation; she joins divine Philosophy (a lesser branch of which is astronomy) with divine poetry (inspiration to sing of celestial matters); in the synthesis she effects between these two figures and herself, she reminds again that all forms of wisdom, studied or inspired, active or passive, emanate from the single source. Lastly, in her own loving inclining over the created World, she indicates more intimately than any other figure how all these divine wisdoms descend continually from heaven to men. Here indeed we might see visibly some projection of God's loving care over his creatures, or his providence. God's wisdom was reflected first in his Creation, next in his providential reordering of human life after the Fall. An open book is a standard emblem attribute of Wisdom. The closed and untitled books mysteriously hugged to themselves by 'Urania's' *putti* suggest the more hidden and secret ways of God's wisdom—reinforcing our sense that in this scene are involved aspects of the divine wisdom and Providence—those themes which Milton will later hope to Justify.

CHAPTER III

Paradise Lost: Cosmos, Contemplation, Urania

With that, I think, we may be better placed to turn to the cosmos of *Paradise Lost*, to Milton's 'Urania', and to his four Invocations. Raphael's Stanza led me to think of Milton; and Milton may also lead us back to Raphael, helping us to see how earlier periods perceived the Stanza's *imagini.* I would suggest that Milton's memories of Raphael, in some cases (such as the more visual instances in Book III) perhaps conscious, may be reflected in *Paradise Lost* in the presence not only of specific themes from the Stanza (which he and Raphael could have held in common) but in, evidently, the use of a similar dynamics; and not merely in his reconstruction in poetry of similar iconographic motifs and details to those on the Stanza's vault and walls, but of corresponding clusters of such. I do not suggest that Milton employed any total programme either of quite such intricacy or such regular balances as Raphael's: although he would certainly have appreciated its subtle modulations, its blendings of lesser schemes into a dominant scheme, and on the whole, I think, would have been in sympathy with what the Stanza was trying to say. Even in the Stanza, it is in the nature of the *imagini* that they retain a numinousness, defy complete analysis: and that is how recollections (if they are such) surface in *Paradise Lost.* Nor am I suggesting that Milton reused every motif on the Stanza's vault and walls. Some he would have found particularly congenial, while others, for his own reasons, he would have omitted. And quite obviously, Milton would have adapted as well as adopted, inflecting Raphael's not entirely 'unconform' pre-Tridentine theology and earlier Renaissance humanism in directions closer to both Protestant doctrinal emphasis and to Milton's own particular theology, incorporating also some conventions and themes from the traditions of Christian narrative poetry and Christian epic preceding *Paradise Lost.* But there still seem to me to be both some very striking correspondences and, in other instances, some highly intriguing analogies, between *Paradise Lost* and the design and themes of the Stanza.

There is, first, the theme of Contemplation or rapture, rather conspicuous throughout the central Books from III to VIII as well as in the Invocations, and with which Milton's Urania like Raphael's is closely associated. In this connection I will refer again to the Chigi Chapel as well as to the Stanza. There is, second, the very important problem of the complex persons-or-personalities of Milton's elusive Muse, sometimes named by him (only tentatively) as Urania, but whose identity and exact values seem to shift prismatically, in a manner reminiscent of that compelling three-figured corner of the Stanza ceiling which especially closely links Raphael's Poetry, cosmic 'Urania' and Philosophy. In this context I shall want to refer more closely to 'The Parnassus'. And there are lastly the wider questions raised by the even more drastically modulating values and identities of the several invoked personae (Heavenly Muse—Spirit—Light—goddess, etc.) within each of and also as between all four of Milton's Invocations. These, as everyone knows, are not mere introductions or prefaces but something more basic, standing (it may be) as more particular 'keys' to the main narrative concerns of Milton's epic (as well as introducing the four regions, infernal, celestial, cosmic, and finally earthly, of his cosmic geography) and providing a kind of quartering, integration and designation which evidently is unique to *Paradise Lost* and atypical of traditional epic. It seems to me also that within each Invocation (although more distinctly in the first three than in the fourth) we witness through the modulations a very similar kind of 'descent' from heavenly powers to earthly to that which is conveyed by the downward connection of each of Raphael's celestial figures in the ceiling globes (and associated figures in the rectangles) with the more comprehensive terrestrial scenes depicted on the wall immediately below her. That is to say, there is a similar expansion ('amplificatio') from the concentrated iconography of divine virtù into a wider, freer-ranging 'narrative' ensuing. In this connection it will be helpful to look closely at 'The Disputà'. And that lastly we can witness, as between all four Invocations, a similar overlapping and finally merging of the several divine identities invoked, whose personalities, because of continual overlappings, reiterations and shifts from one into another and back again, seem to achieve an ultimate synthesis or concordance comparable to that effected in the 'summing-up' in the four-personned ceiling of Raphael's celestial cycle, the four main figures revolving endlessly around and merging in their heavenly central focus: a synthesis which, as in Raphael, affords a constant divine orientation for the human concerns more diffusely depicted 'below'. It is tempting to think that there are in the Milton the same two complementary directions of movement that we find in the Stanza: a descent within each separate Invocation from divine to human; coupled with reconciliation or synthesis, sweeping broadly across the poem from Invocation to Invocation, with their repeating but always somewhat differently stressed *personae.*

More specific discussion of *Paradise Lost* is now indicated. I turn first to the theme of Contemplation: contemplation not initially of the divine but, as a first step, of the '*visible* diurnal sphere', with the Wonder that such Contemplation evokes.

> In contemplation of created things
> By steps we may ascend to God. . . .
> (V. 511-12)[1]

Adam's echo of Raphael's earlier exposition of the *Scala Naturae* is also emblematized earlier in *Paradise Lost* in the Golden Stairs let down from Heaven (III. 501-25), which Satan is briefly allowed to see, and each step of which has a mystic meaning ('mysteriously was meant'): that is, takes men one stage further up the ladder to God. Contemplation of created things (especially of the shining heavens by God's creatures so as to lead them back to Him) is an activity conducted with satisfaction by the Creator also—the whole 'process' implying a circularity, process or emanation and return, alternatively descent and reascent, which is again summed up by Raphael in another passage in Book V:

> O *Adam*, one Almightie is, from whom
> All things proceed, and up to him return . . .
> (V. 469 ff)

Contemplation of the created cosmos is a basic, accepted activity in Milton's world. It provides the excuse which Satan offers to Uriel for appearing, disguised as a stripling Cherub, on the Sun in Book III. 660-67: exactly that, that he has come to *wonder* at the new creation (he uses the word twice, and it recurs). Almost the first 'personal' conversation of Adam and Eve in Book IV, following immediately after the biblically-inspired accounts by Adam of the Prohibition and by Eve of her creation, concerns the stars, which they must be contemplating as they walk in the evening. But such contemplation by creatures is a second stage, in effect, of the two-way process alluded to above: for the first instance of contemplation which we are given in *Paradise Lost* pertains to God himself. As Book III opens, he,

> High Thron'd above all highth, bent down his eye,
> His own works and their works at once to view . . .
> (III. 58-59)

One view: which takes in all, from the inconceivable height. That divine sweep is traditional, of course (it is also in Tasso);[2] but the especially dizzying perspective achieved by Milton is an 'illusionist' effect (the double perspective) such as we find in our view of God seen from below in the Chigi Chapel, or more especially that which we can imagine as seen by God himself from above.

An amplified view of that divine perspective is seen in greater detail, shortly, by Satan at the next stage of his false inquiry: seen at the very place where the golden stairs lead (or should lead) men back to God. Satan

> Looks down with wonder at the sudden view
> Of all this World at once...
>
> (III. 542 ff.)

The sensation of wonder is conveyed not so much by particulars of the actual view as by simile (the wonderful simile of discovery, "As when a Scout...," III. 540-44); the sense of vertiginous cosmic depths into which Satan is looking; and finally, the crazily impossible angle from which *we* appear to be sighting *him*. Satan's own exhilaration and rapture are conveyed in the sense of speed in his plunge "Down right into the Worlds first Region" (III. 562—we have a satellite view of him gliding past the planets), the ease with which he "sailes between worlds and worlds" (to borrow from Raphael's similar flight in Book V. 268), and the sheer exhilaration of the "many an Aerie wheele" into which he "throws his steep flight" (III. 741) before landing on the Sun. There the motif of 'wonder' returns explicitly: "So *wondrously* was set his Station bright" (III. 587). That sense is reaffirmed after Satan lands on the top of Eden's mount and looks down: "Beneath him with *new wonder* now he views... exposed..." (IV. 205). What Milton describes in such passages, the sensation Satan feels or we might feel at first sight of such a brave new World, the painter can achieve with an expression and a gesture: the almost astonished rapture registered on the face of Raphael's 'Urania' and by her hand flung back, as she too gazes down into the star-sprinkled depths of the cosmos below her. In such descriptions as these, or in the resemblances between Satan's position in Space and that of God the Father in the Chigi Chapel, or in the Jacob's Vision scene (another parallel presently discussed), one is tempted to find direct visual recollections of Raphael. The possibility seems the stronger, in view of the fact that all the paintings involved were so well known; and that Milton's cosmic views and flights in Book III are so remarkably visual, particular and perspectived.

A parallel interesting moment occurs when Milton's own Raphael, ready to fly down and straining to discern his destination, observes directly below him, that is, in the centre of the cosmos, 'unobstructed', since "no cloud, or, . . . / Starr interpos'd", "a cloudy *spot*" which is "Earth" (V. 257-67). That too is remarkably like the Raphael 'Urania's' orrery, which has a darkish circle at its centre within which is what could be a 'spot' called 'earth'.[3] It is, incidentally, no cause for surprise that Satan's view should expand upon and echo God's own (or that the archangel Raphael's view and flight should re-echo Satan's): for 'perversion' of the good into bad, and redirection of that perverted usage back to the good, are the constant thematic and structural oppositions on which Milton's poem turns.

Satan's first situation previously was on the outermost shell or

firm opacous Globe
Of this round World, whose first convex divides
The luminous inferior Orbs, enclos'd . . .
(III. 418-20)

This locates him as in a position corresponding with Raphael's 'Urania': that is, on the *primum mobile* or 'first convex'—not Heaven, but the closest point of all the created universe or spheres to Heaven (hence here the Golden Stairs). Milton stresses the solidity and also the *opaqueness* ("opacous") of that 'convex' shell or 'globe' as seen by *Satan*: for Satan it permits no through vision (in this his view is unlike God's or the Archangel's 'unobstructed' views). Raphael's 'Urania', by contrast, leans on the outer globe as if it were solid in the way that Satan perceives it: but for her it is transparent (since we see right through the orrery to the outlines of the lower part of her body at the farther side). Perhaps for her this 'shell' is 'glassy'—like the 'sea of glass' in *Rev.* 4. 6, rendered by Milton as the "cleer *Hyaline*, the Glassie Sea" (VII. 619) or, in Book III, the sea of "liquid Pearle" across which Elijah "flew ore the Lake / Rapt in a Chariot drawn by fiery Steeds" (III. 519; 521-22).

How can Satan answer this rather human problem of how to see into the opacous globe? Being in fact fallen and so like us, he seeks the kind of solution we might—he hunts around for an opening in the solid shell and presently finds one: "a passage wide" (III. 528) at the foot of the Golden Stairs, one used also by the angels (cf. Jacob's vision, III. 510-12) as they ascend and descend between heaven and earth. It is against this aperture or hole that we, looking upward, have that breathtakingly foreshortened view of Satan straddled above us—perhaps the single most unforgettable visual image in *Paradise Lost.* Highly painterly in the illusionist or baroque manner of the sixteenth century, achieving impossible perspectives, the picture shown to us is of Satan from almost directly *underneath,* yet at the same time it embraces his own view down into the cosmos:

> Round he surveys, and well might, where he stood
> So high above the circling Canopie
> Of Nights extended shade; from Eastern Point
> Of *Libra* to the fleecie Starr that bears
> *Andromeda* farr off *Atlantick* Seas
> Beyond th'Horizon; then from Pole to Pole
> He views in bredth...
>
> (III. 555-61)

Satan's location and such a perspective as he and we achieve seems to me extraordinarily reminiscent of that looming upward nigh impossible view of God seen from the floor of the Chigi Chapel, framed against the opening of the cupola, so foreshortened as to make it seem as if we are looking at him almost upside down. (It will be recalled that the effect of sharp edges framing an opening into Heaven was also connected with the central roundel of the Stanza vault.) 'Urania' on the Stanza vault is a little comparable, inasmuch as she too is seen as if the spectator were placed a little below her. It is interesting that there is a further association with the Chigi Chapel in Milton's allusion to Elijah being carried to heaven: the altar of the Chapel is flanked on the right by a statue of Elijah (to Raphael's design, but not added to the chapel until late). Elijah is looking up with an expression indicative of inspiration or inward 'seeing'.[4] Presumably these two subjects (the Spheres and Elijah) were traditionally associated and so used by both Milton and Raphael. It is also interesting to note that the zodiacal signs alluded to in Satan's grandiose sweep of the eyes, Libra, the Ram and Andromeda, are with other signs of the zodiac presented in the smaller half-spheres, with attendant angels, circling the base of the Chigi dome. Here too one may, by turning the head, see 'across' the breadth of the universe, from Libra's eastern scales to the 'fleecy star' (the Ram) who 'bears Andromeda beyond the horizon'.[5]

One further remarkable parallel to Raphael in the cosmic parts of Book III connects not with the Segnatura but with the adjacent Stanza, the Eliodoro and its vault. In a highly dramatic composition, there is painted on one of the four segments of the vault a picture, almost life-size, of Jacob dreaming his vision of the Golden Stairs to Heaven. The picture is unusually framed in one of the odd-shaped, elongated spaces provided by the diagonal axes of the vault's X-shaped design. Jacob lies stretched out on the ground (his body filling most of the lower part of the space), his head pillowed on his scrip, under a sky of deepest midnight blue. To his right are the golden stairs (foreshortened), on which a busy traffic is seen of preoccupied angels, of great beauty, hurriedly ascending and descending, intent on their various errands. 'At top whereof' is the entrance to Heaven, and God. (No 'kingly palace gate', however.) The scene seems to be closely reflected in Milton's lines describing the same scene (lines 510-15, falling between the two cosmic views of Satan at 418-22 and 555-61). Milton's passage runs:

> The Stairs were such as whereon *Jacob* saw
> Angels ascending and descending, bands
> Of Guardians bright, when he from *Esau* fled
> To *Padan-Aram* in the field of *Luz*,
> Dreaming by night under the open Skie,
> And waking cri'd, This is the Gate of Heav'n.

Milton's lines seem to catch the very spirit of Raphael's painting: especially in that detail of 'dreaming by night under the open sky'.[6]

To turn to Milton's Muse. His Urania (like Raphael's figure) also is associated with the visible spheres and with divine contemplation. But whereas Raphael's 'Urania' 'contemplates' in tranquil rapture, caught as if in arrested motion, and is herself specifically not winged, Milton's figure of (presumably) the same name belongs with the spheres and also flies high above them. She is clearly cosmic, since she is called on specifically in Book VII, the macroscosmic part of the poem, and directs or supports those dazzling stellar flights described in the poet's imagination. She goes *beyond* the cosmic spheres however, in that she physically (as it were) transports the poet through Hell and Chaos, "through utter and through middle darkness borne" (III. 16), "down / The dark descent, and up... Though hard and rare" (III. 19-21), then (like Elijah) "Into the Heav'n of Heav'ns" and "with like safetie.... down" again, so that he is "Standing on Earth, not rapt above the Pole" (VII. 13, 15, 23). 'Rapture' is the etymological pun (and possibly in Raphael too is a visual 'conceit') which forces the narrative and intellectual links between passively wondering contemplation; being physically caught up on high or flying; the winged flights of poetic inspiration; and prophetic inspiration such as Elijah's—all of which are subsumed in the passages at Book III. 520-60 and in the Invocations to Books III and VII. 'Rapture' such as in the Miltonic Urania's song or her flights; or in

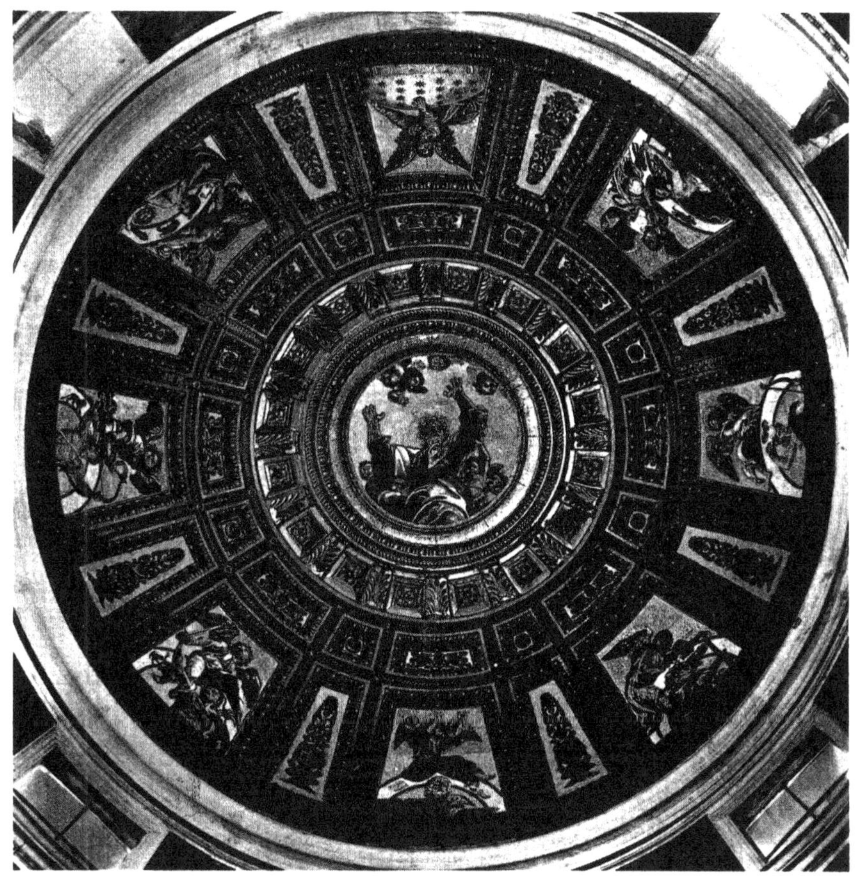

Raphael: mosaic dome and cupola, Chigi Chapel, S. Maria del Popolo, Rome.

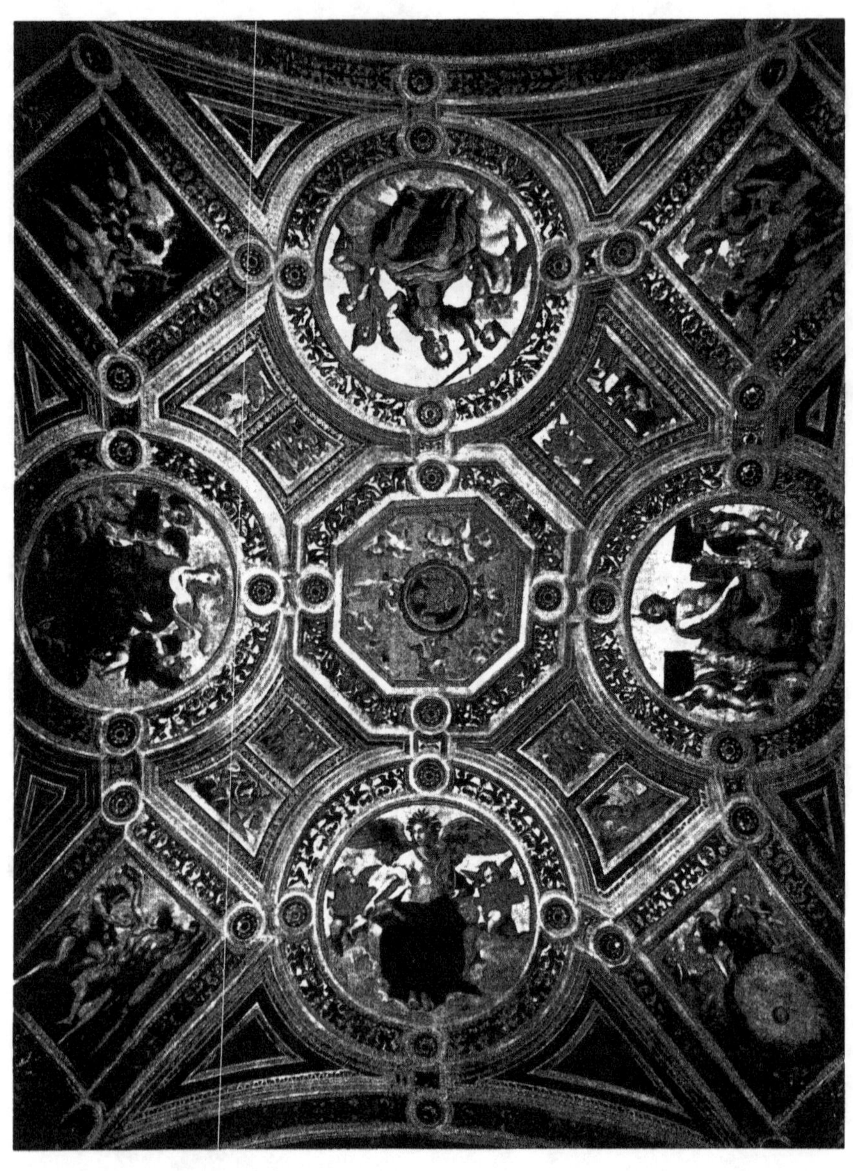

Raphael: vault of Stanza della Segnatura, Vatican.

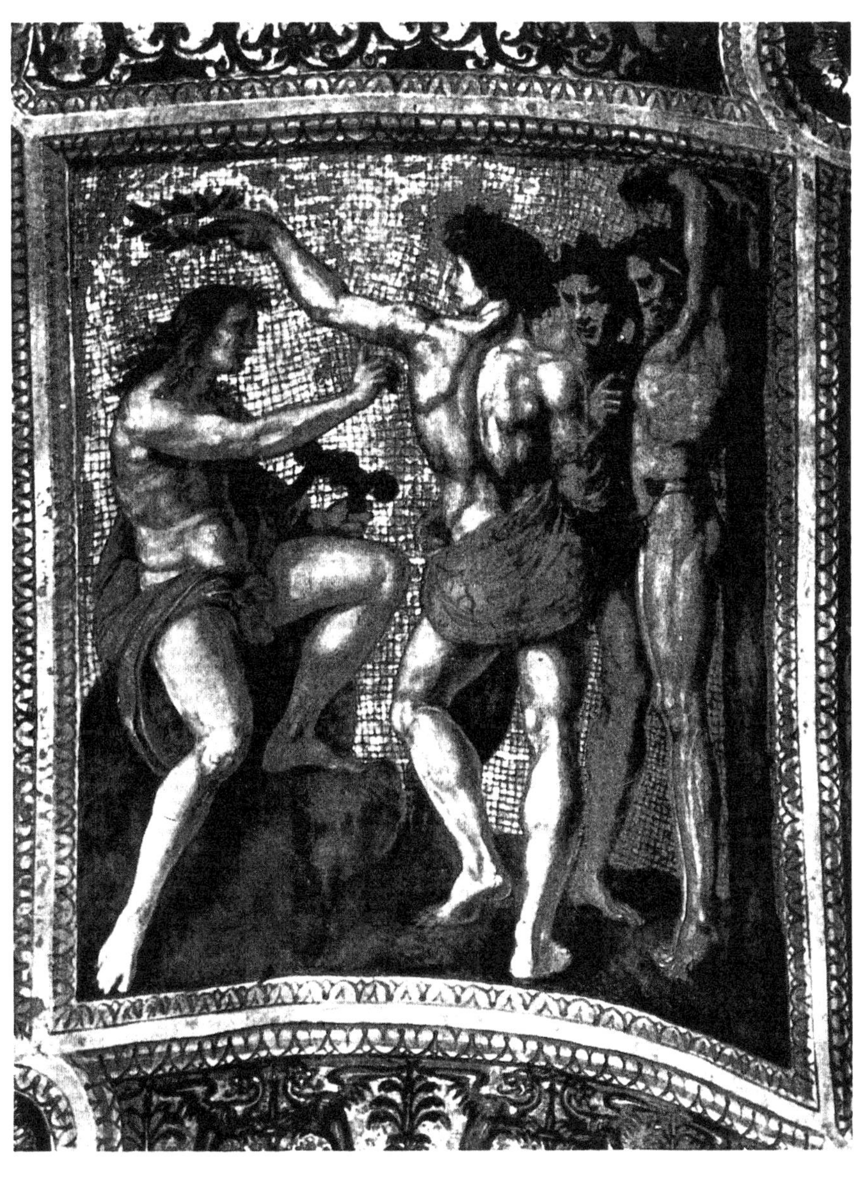

Raphael: Marsyas and Apollo (detail).

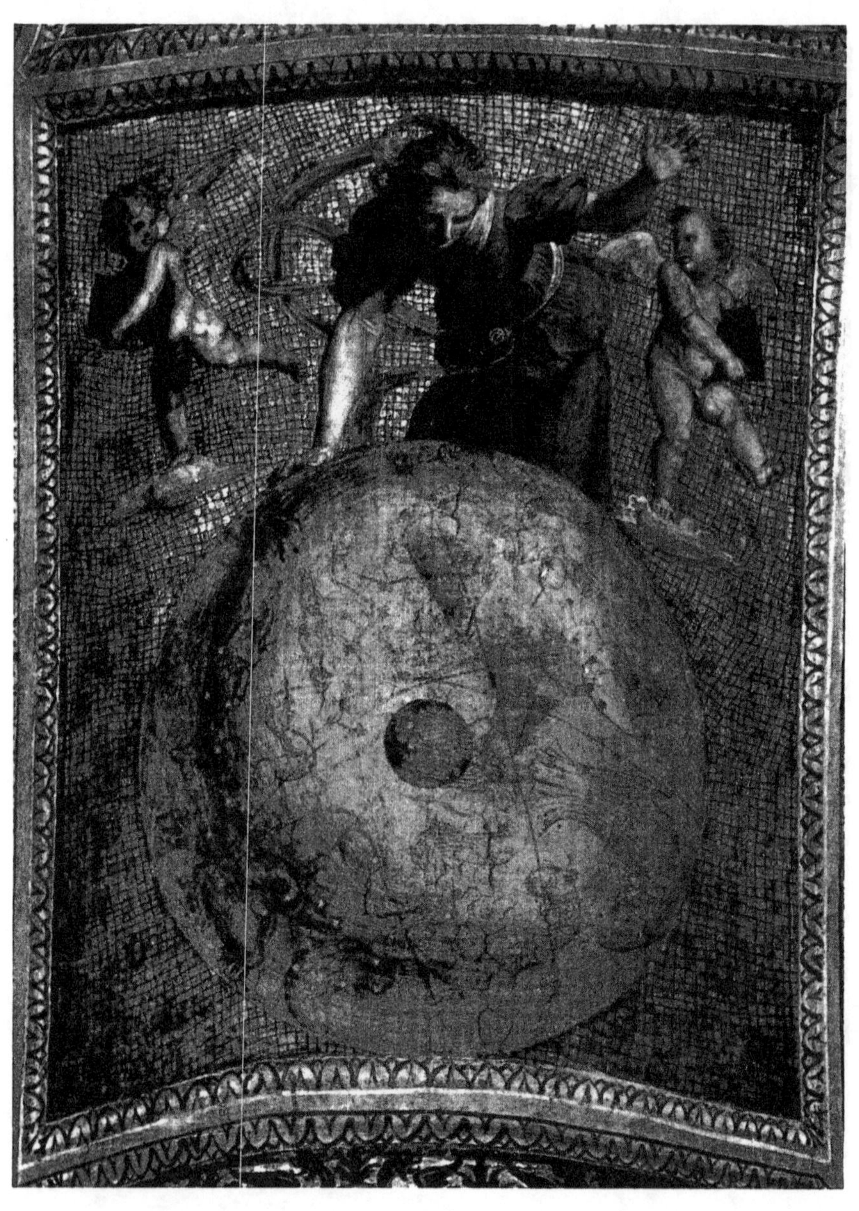

Raphael: 'Urania' (detail).

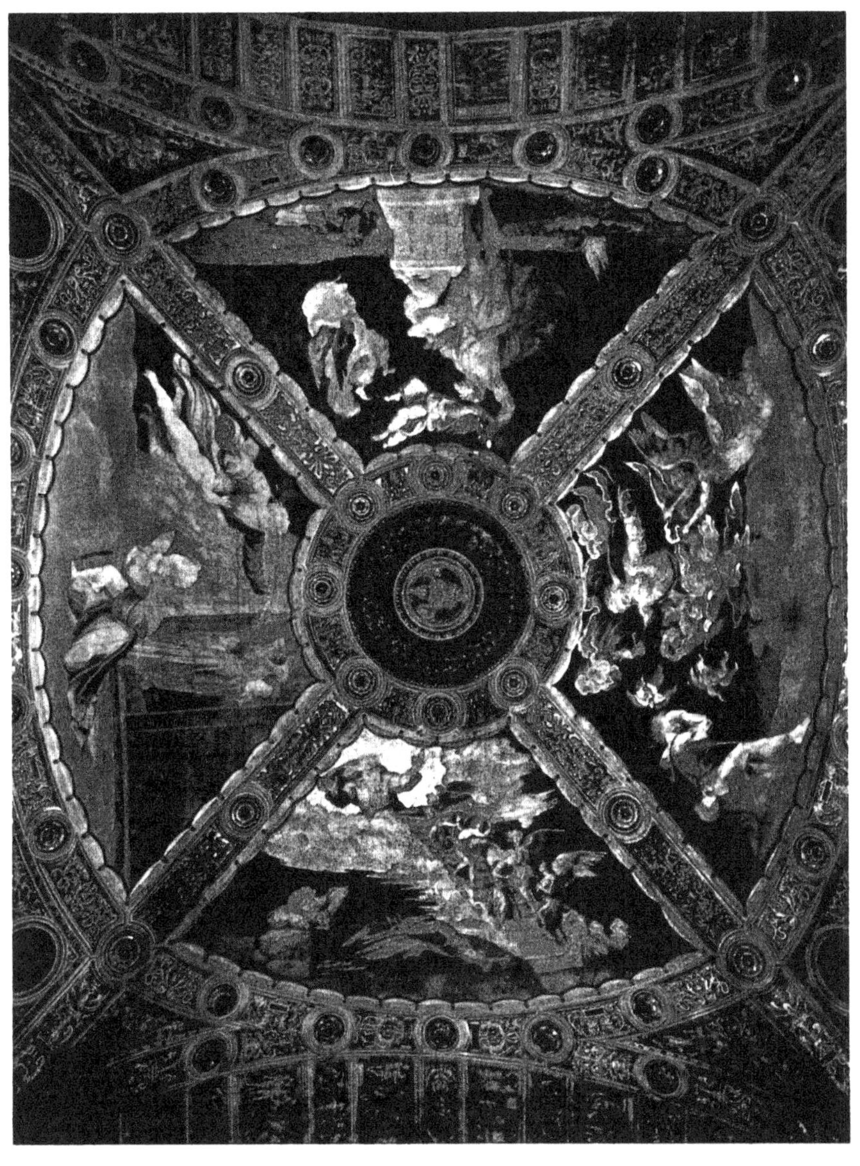

Raphael: vault of Stanza d'Eliodoro (including Jacob's Dream), Vatican.

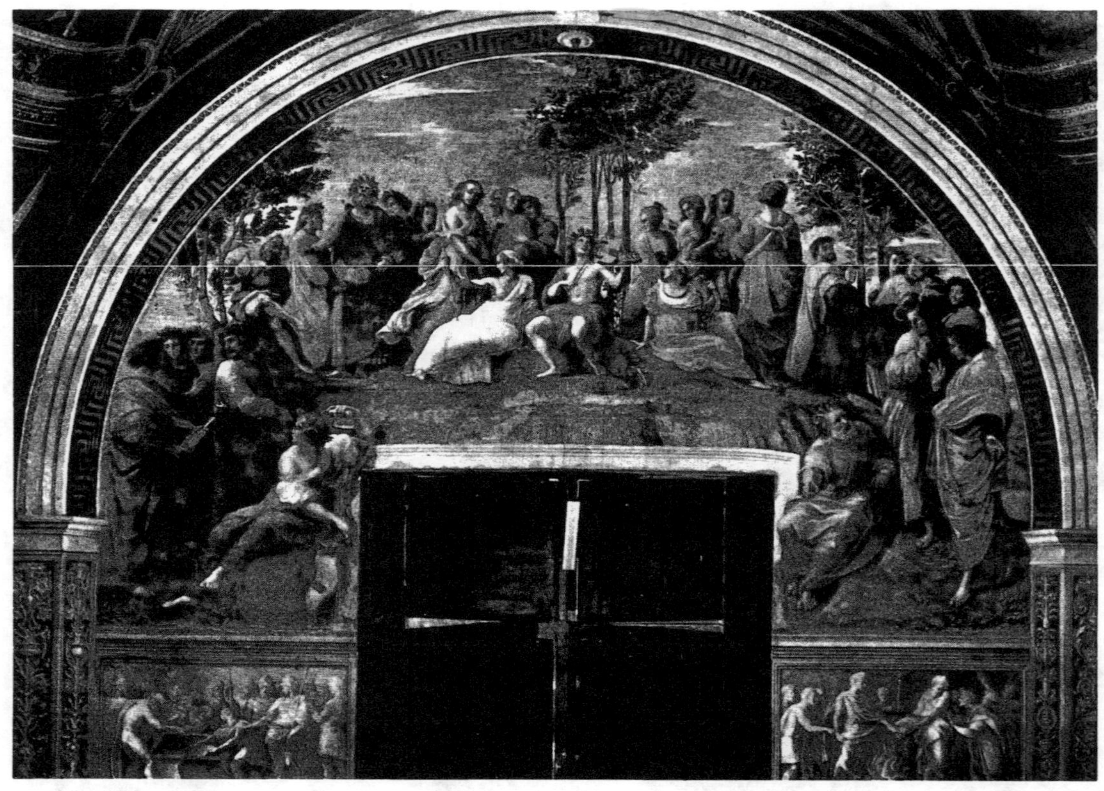

Raphael: Parnassus, Stanza della Segnatura, Vatican.

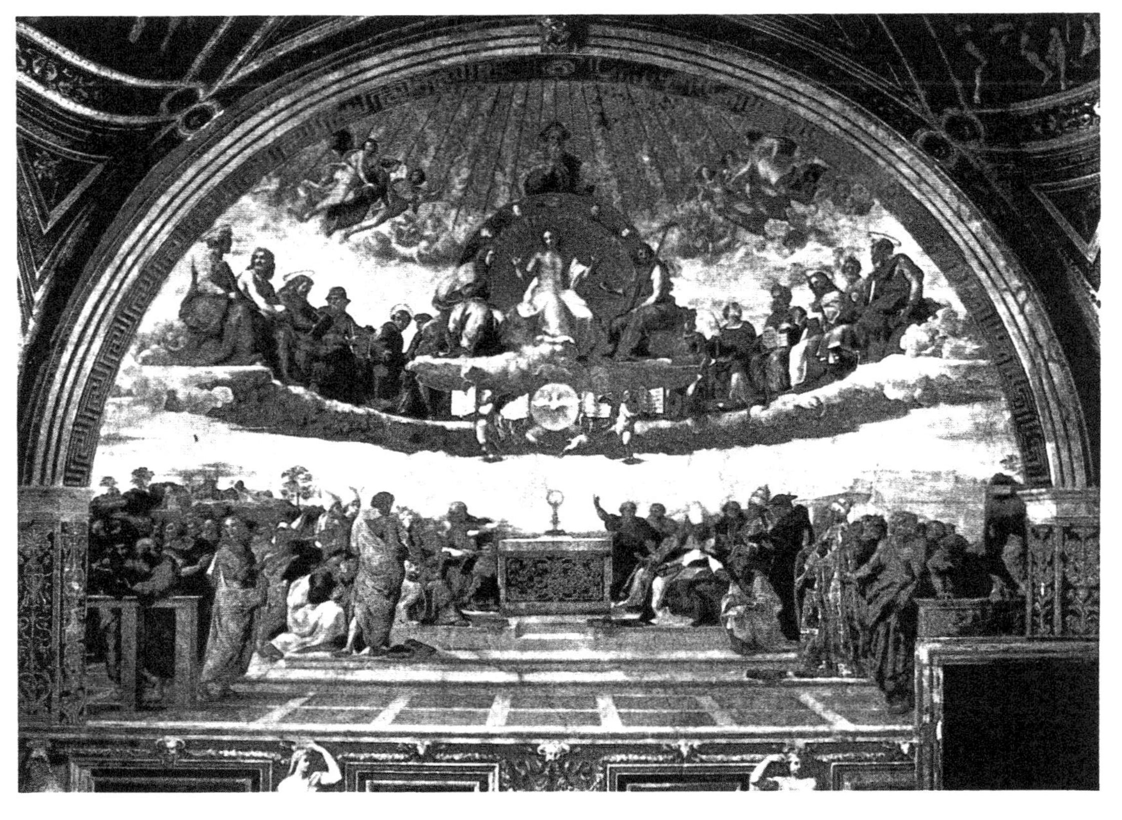

Raphael: Disputà, Stanza della Segnatura, Vatican.

ASTROLOGIE.

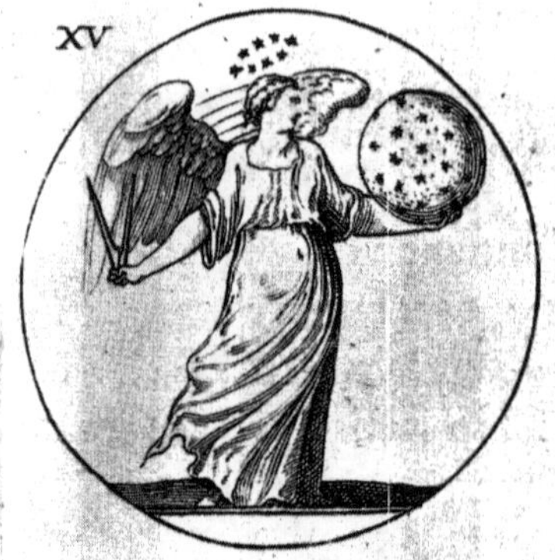

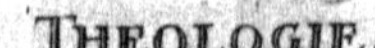

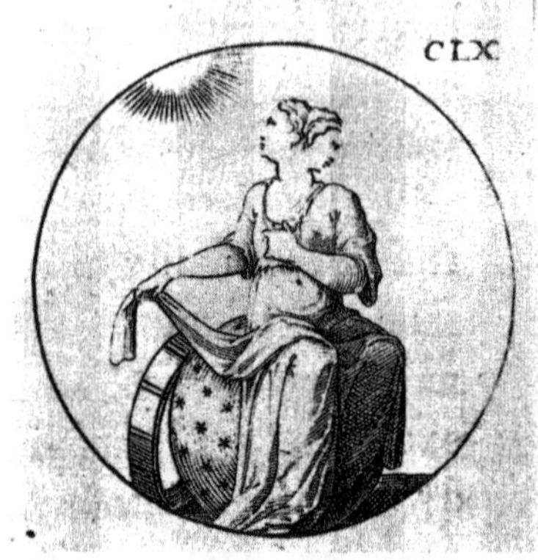

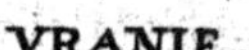

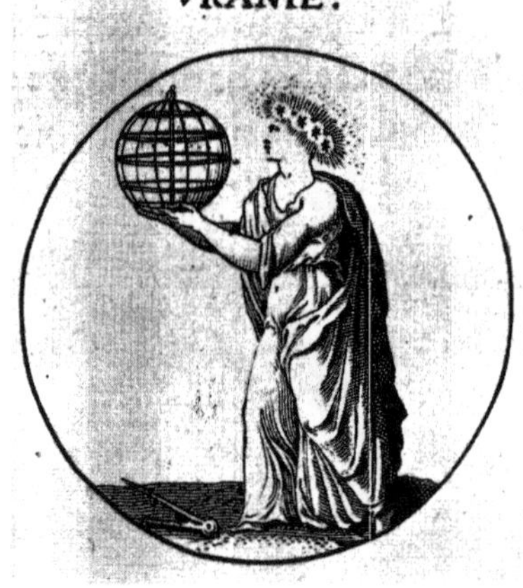

POESIE.

CXXXII

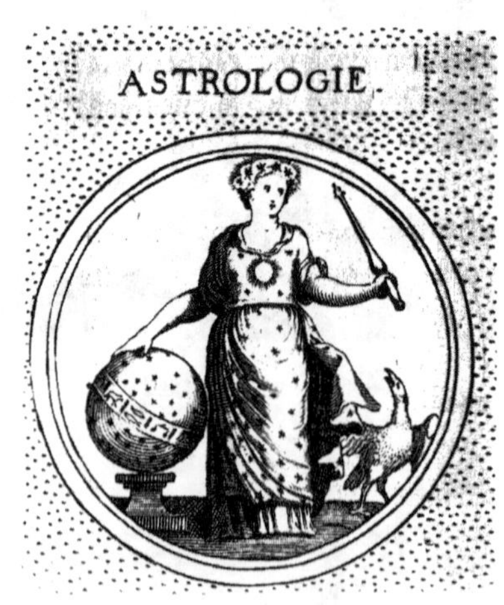

Cesare Ripa, Emblems. From ed. J. Baudouin, *Iconologie* (1677).

Satan's 'wonder' when gazing down at the World; or violent *transport* (itself a pun) such as in the poet's (or Satan's) situation "rapt above the pole"[7] or Elijah rapt in a fiery chariot (of course both metaphors of flight, poetic or prophetic, are also figures for inward inspiration or 'rapture')—all such meanings superimpose. Such linked senses of 'rapt' / 'rapture' recur throughout especially the Book VII Invocation (the first direct naming of Urania). We have here all the modulations of flight; contemplation of the spheres; rapture; poetic transport; song: "Descend from Heav'n *Urania*"; "above th'*Olympian* Hill I *soare*"; "whose *Voice* divine / Following"; "*rapt* above the *Pole*"; "more safe I *Sing*" (VII, 1-3; 23-24); then the figure of the poet-priest Orpheus: "Woods and rocks had Eares / To *rapture*" (VII. 35-36).

In this last connection: I wonder if Milton uses the figure of Orpheus, the poet-priest who is torn to pieces, as a kind of equivalent for the Marsyas-Apollo motif employed in a parallel context in the Stanza? Both Marsyas-Apollo and Orpheus are musicians, and semi-divine figures. Orpheus, like Marsyas-Apollo, represents simultaneously two opposite sides of the same: bodily-spiritual-anguish, and inspiration-rapture-glory. The two myths do seem to have some kind of overlapping valency in the Renaissance; although it is the Orpheus legend which has the clearer history of Christian allegorization.[8]

The reference to *Moses* in Invocation Book I, and the specific association of poets with prophets in Invocation Book III. 35-36 (also we remember Elijah later in Book III), and of all ancient poets or prophets with Milton himself (34), followed immediately afterward by the advent of his own poetic inspiration (36-37), reinforce the idea that all are bound up with inward contemplation ("Then feed on thoughts...", III. 37). Outward blindness, as of Thamyris and Maeonides and Milton, is an old figure for inner sight: blind Homer appears on Raphael's Parnassian hill. It is to such concurrences of motifs and personae in the Miltonic Invocations, and their links with 'contemplation' and with cosmic flights through the spheres which are Urania's domain, or higher still, that I want for the moment to draw attention: and to the fact that similar concatenations occur not only in the one corner of the Stanza vault, but elsewhere in the Stanza (as on the Parnassus hill).

It can be seen (as already in the poetic inspiration-contemplation allusions) that Milton's Urania like Raphael's is complex, ambivalent and not to be restricted to that deity or science which 'puts the stars... in their appointed places'. Milton in Book VII specifically dissociates his Muse from the astronomical Muse—or any other: "thou / Nor of the

Muses nine, nor on the top / Of old *Olympus* dwellst" (5-7). He also seems to go out of his way to raise doubts over the identity of his own Urania—if indeed she has any *one* 'identity' or 'name'—in that arresting opening to Book VII:

> Descend from Heav'n *Urania, by that name*
> *If rightly thou art calld*

For it is the "meaning, not the Name" Milton calls upon, in fact invokes: neither a named deity nor a personification but something deeper, some divine essence: a Urania who is "Heav'nlie borne". Further, she *preceded* the Creation and is or nearly is in some way co-eternal with God:

> Before the hills appeerd, or Fountain flowd,
> Thou with Eternal wisdom didst converse

We might suppose Eternal Wisdom to be God; but then it appears that she is in fact a rather perplexing sister to Urania:

> Thou with Eternal wisdom didst converse,
> Wisdom thy Sister, and with her didst play
> In presence of th'almightie Father, pleas'd
> With thy Celestial Song.
> (VII. 1-12)

There has been so much critical anxiety spent over the identity of Milton's Urania and the meaning of the above passage in particular that it would be unprofitable to renew all the arguments.[9] We can note, however, that the Urania figure of Book VII (not unlike the 'Urania' of Raphael's vault) is not very far removed in presence from God; she has a 'sister'—Wisdom—who is 'eternal'; and she 'plays' in God's *presence* (although not thereby exactly made co-identical with Him). But somehow also before the passage finishes, she has been brought round once again to *Poetry* or divine Poetry: God is 'pleased with her *celestial song*'—this is the divine *Muse* who earlier and presently again soars high.

It may be thought, then, that in the Milton configuration or conflation of Wisdom (eternal)-Urania (cosmic contemplation and rapture)-winged Poetry (inspiration), we have something very like the expanded visual conceit in the first corner of the Stanza vault, that which knits 'Urania' as the Universe or divine Contemplation of it on her either side to divine Poetry and divine Wisdom ('Knowledge of Causes'): all three heavenly, all three wedded, all three forms of wisdom emanating from a single divine source. And if Milton's like Raphael's Urania partly embodies God's contemplation of 'his own works', then the words which

Milton appends, "His own works *and their works* at once to view" (III. 59), quite naturally extends that activity from space into time, from Contemplation to Providence. That is to say, God's contemplation of things visible or present extends into his providence or knowledge of things not visible or future (an implication which has been detected in the Raphael figure). Milton's *Of Christian Doctrine* has something relevant to say: "the foreknowledge of God is nothing but the wisdom of God, *under another name*, or that idea of every thing, which he had in his mind . . . before he decreed anything".[10] I do not think that Raphael's 'Urania' figure is to be *restricted* to 'Providenzia'—any more than she is to 'Contemplation'. But I believe that Raphael and Milton may both be trying to convey much the same thought. Providence or God's foreknowledge is simply one part of, a more active manifestation of, the eternal Wisdom: just as is God's Contemplation of the created universe. God's "Eternal Providence" (His wisdom, in fact) is the subject exactly of Milton's poem and of the song his heavenly Muse is committed to sing. Yet how can either divine Contemplation or divine Providence (any more than poetic or prophetic wisdom directly inspired) be ultimately separable from "Eternal wisdom": or any of these from "th'almightie Father" himself—other than, of course (as Milton himself indicates), through a variety of poetical personifications[11] (as, in Raphael, through a variety of iconographical representations)—that is, through distinctions merely verbal or visual?[12] All these aspects of Wisdom are aspects of the same, 'under another name'. And it is inner *meaning*, ultimately simple and single, not *names*, with which Milton is concerned. However, we have perhaps taken this particular Miltonic and Raphaelesque symbiosis—Poetry, Urania (in her several aspects), Philosophy—as far as is profitable. In both artists they all three appear as intertwined: all are aspects of the divine wisdom, 'personified' as Milton says under a variety of names. All therefore flow into each other numinously and unbrokenly: in the 'presiding' Ladies of the globes and the Urania rectangle; in Milton's Invocations. That seems to be their point.

CHAPTER IV

Paradise Lost: Invocations, 'Parnassus', 'Disputà'

What we can do, less speculatively, is turn to two of Raphael's wall paintings, both to compare and confirm the theme of 'descent' in the *Paradise Lost* Invocations, referred to earlier, and to illustrate more closely the ways in which Milton's divine poetic Muse and her rôles seem to be aligned with Raphael's. I shall comment on two wall frescoes, the first 'The Parnassus'. Raphael's figure of Poetry, as has been said, sits crowned with laurel above the clouds, holding her lyre and her book, her wings extended to the full, flanked by her *putti* and tablets, the "numine afflatur" on the Stanza vault. Gombrich stresses the importance of the fact that she sits directly *above* the Hill of Parnassus, which is the subject of the entire wall below. In the centre of this picture, at the top of a gentle hill and at the foot of a little grove of trees, Apollo seated plays (his instrument resembling a viol) to the nine Muses, who are grouped immediately either side of him (five and four). The Castalian spring is visible as a small spring-head, between Apollo and the first Muse. Among them is the lesser Urania, seated on the ground and gazing (as tradition has it) past Apollo and up at the Heavens.[1] Apollo's eyes are also looking upward, but rather to the centre top of the painting: as if toward that place where divine Poetry presides. It is as if Apollo mutely seeks, invokes, his 'celestial Patroness': acknowledges that his inspiration comes from on high. Poetry in the *tondo* above him seems half to acknowledge him in return. As has been said, her right arm (the one holding the book) is extended in a direction which carries the line obliquely toward the group below; her head too inclines down, although her eyes are delphically directed into unknown distances—as if in contemplation of invisible things. To either side of the group on the Parnassus stand, in more energetic postures, famous poets of the classical past and European tradition extending into the near present. They include quite unmistakeably blind Homer (also Dante) as well as many other older or modern figures who have with less or greater certainty been identified.[2]

It is tempting to think that this is the composition Milton remembers in the lines:

> Yet not the more
> Cease I to wander where the Muses haunt
> Cleer Spring, or shadie Grove, or Sunnie Hill
> (III. 26-28)

The hill of Parnassus, with its spring, grove, open space and the Muses; all surmounted by the imposing single figure high above on the ceiling *tondo*. He calls for help to "soar / *Above* th' *Aonian* Mount" (I. 15); or again "*above* th'*Olympian* Hill" and "*Above* the flight of *Pegasean* wing" (VII. 3; 4). What he then must also specifically be recollecting is, surmounting this very gentle Parnassian "hill" (the word is appropriate to Raphael's picture as well as to *Paradise Lost*), the commanding winged figure of Poetry in the *tondo* above: seated, but with strong wings stretched out and well able to "soar". Like Raphael, Milton makes the point overwhelmingly that the Muse on whom he 'calls' is divine and not one of the pagan nine: "Whose Voice *divine* / Following, above th'*Olympian* Hill I soare" (VII. 2-3). Her authority, being divine, is far greater. She is *not* to be confused with those ancient Muses who attended on the Greek gods:

> thou
> Nor of the Muses nine, nor on the top
> Of old *Olympus* dwellst, but Heav'nlie borne
> (VII. 5-7)

And more severely,

> nor could the Muse defend
> Her Son . . . .
> For *thou art Heav'nlie*, shee an empty dreame.
> (VII. 37-39)

If Milton stresses the superiority of his own divine Muse to the poetic fiction of the Parnassian group, nothing equally could be more plainly displayed by the entire disposition and attitudes of the figures on the Raphael Parnassus compared with the Poetry above them. The figure on the *tondo* is tense, poised and commanding; those reclining on the hill far less dynamic, indeed rather languid, meditative, dreamy (might one say, dream*like*; *fictive*?).

Although the Parnassian Muses may have something of the quality of an idle dream, Raphael's human figures of poets to the right and left of them and extending down round the foot of the hill are extremely real: historical. Some are recognizable. All are shown doing something: gesturing, conversing, or at least *looking* purposeful. This is the real world. And each group of poets, to right and left, has its own little smaller grove: details here, as in the upper part of 'The Parnassus', quite closely matching those in Milton's first and third Invocations. Homer is conspicuous: rapt, blind, his sightless but 'seeing' eyes turned up to Heaven. Milton could, did, see himself there among them: at any rate, he certainly bracketed himself with Homer and other blind poets and prophets in that 'shady grove' or on the 'sunny hill'.

Obviously, Milton, while dismissing the religious authority of the pagan Muses (and of course their historical existence—but who ever thought them 'real'?) is not thereby dismissing the idea of the dependence of human poets upon inspiration or divine inspiration: nor the longed-for, prayed-for but almost unlooked-for ways in which it can suddenly 'descend'. His Invocations, in this respect, say much what the Raphael *tondo* and its wall say: that men always must depend upon the divine *afflatus* and that *it* descends (as and when it chooses) down to *them*. (The 'waiting', the expectancy, the involuntariness, are all beautifully evoked in *Paradise Lost*, III. 25-40 and IX. 20-25.)

However, one point must strike us about Raphael's Poetry-Parnassus configuration (if it has not already), with respect to Milton's. The conspicuously winged figure presiding in the *tondo* is, as has been said, that of Poetry: and so it is she seemingly (and not the 'Urania' figure) who is being recalled by Milton as the diviner Muse of his evoking, able to fly high 'above the Olympian hill'. Yet Milton's own Muse is nevertheless (if uncertainly) called *Urania*—the figure who arguably is Raphael's enraptured lady leaning down over the starry spheres. I think that by now there is little needed to explain this seeming discrepancy. Raphael's own somewhat differently presented but equally mysterious symbiosis of Poetry-Urania (both cognate to Philosophy or divine Wisdom) in that first corner of the Stanza vault represents very much the same kind of semi-mystic conflation that Milton is making. (Literary traditions, to which I shall return later, also do something to explain the particular conjunction of Poetry-Urania-cosmic Muse; and the conflation is also reflected in at least one emblem, described in Appendix III, which shows a winged 'Astrology'.) The 'Urania' of *Paradise Lost*—as indeed of Raphael—pointedly retains her close associations with the "visible Diurnal Spheare" (VII. 22) and her place "above the starrie Sphear" (III. 416). But considering her much enlarged meaning or meanings, it seems possible that it was especially the three-fold *concetto* on the Stanza vault, with its striking visual approximation of the three celestially interrelated Ladies, that might have been retained by Milton in the mind's eye, that eye 'planted' inward: till later the mind, "through all her powers / Irradiate[d]" (III. 52-53), could once again bring forward and reformulate the old *imagini*. We may also be struck by how self-consciously Milton in Book VII deploys the 'pagan' motif ("*Urania*... Say *Goddess*...", 31; 40)—although it is of course implicitly Christianized—side by side with the most elevated of Christian themes ("Th'almightie Father", "Eternal wisdom", earlier). This constant paralleling of classical and Christian motifs is itself one of the most constant and striking features of the Stanza's message.

To return to the theme of 'descent'. The kind of 'descent' which we see in Raphael's Stanza—from the celestial down to the inward, personal and then more widely human—Milton epitomizes in that unforgettable opening to Book VII: "Descend from Heav'n *Urania*...". The descent Urania is here required to make is in part from heavenly (in Book III) to cosmic and earthly matters in Book VII (the Creation account, which follows after the conclusion of the proem). The indication of the kind of matter over which the Muse will in this section of the poem preside—"Say Goddess, what ensu'd when *Raphael*, / The affable Arch-Angel, had forewarnd / Adam" (VII. 40-42)—illustrates just that kind of *amplificatio*, through the body of Books VII and VIII, from enigmatic *concetto* to extended plain narrative as is exhibited in the way the mystic *imagine* of each Raphael *tondo* 'descends' into the expanded illustrations ('visual narrative') on the walls: the treatment of the subject becoming more and more expansive as, for example, we pass from the higher Parnassus to the flanking lower subjects in their own 'Parnassi'. But first, here as in each Invocation, Milton narrows down to the individual, adds his personal voice. 'Descent' of heavenly powers, then, in Book VII, becomes also the fortitude to sing on in 'evil days'. In at least two other Invocations (Books I and III, and perhaps tentatively also in IX) the same pattern is repeated: the quasi-mystic evocation and invocation of one or more divine impulses or identities, on whom the poet like all men depends for wisdom, instruction, or inspiration; followed by the larger descent of those same powers down into men's lives at large, represented by individuals of the past, as well as in the present by the poet; followed by the further expansion into extended narration. Book IX varies this invocatory pattern: but the 'descent' motif may still be perceived in the prayer for a personal and 'answerable' style to the specific problems of the Christian epic subject. The pattern is just so in the Stanza: Poetry presides not only above the Parnassians but above all poets who have actually lived, past or recent or (probably) present. (It can be seen how the main lines of the group of figures curve from the group on the hilltop down to the sides and round and down again into the more numerous groupings lower.) And just so in the Justice *tondo*: Justice presides, first over her associated Virtues (she has this double aspect), then over her human representatives. And with the Theology figure, who presides first over the amplification in the celestial triptych and flanking Gospels, it widening down into the human 'Disputà'; and again with Philosophy above 'The School of Athens'. (The details of the downward linkages of these celestial figures have been noted.) Each *tondo* figure 'governs' her particular 'subject': just as in Book VII Milton's Urania 'governs' his 'song'. And as with the four main narrative sections of *Paradise Lost*, each fresco on its particular wall extends the single divine impulse down into larger and larger areas of human life, more dispersed groupings and sub-groupings of characters and sub-themes, as the divine impulse diffuses down into all the variety and branches of learning—poetry, divinity, law, philosophy—and human activities depicted below. It is a fairly close equivalent, in visual terms, of Milton's 'amplificatio' from mystic conceit to expanded 'narration'.

'The Disputà' is the visually most dramatic enactment of a celestial descent in the Stanza. This picture is in two parts, rather more distinctly divided than 'The Parnassus'. The upper half of the wall, underlined by a sweeping cloud bank, supports seated figures of alternately Apostles, Evangelists or Saints, and Patriarchs. We can see Moses holding his tablets and David, the author of the Psalms, distinguished by his headdress and his harp, and other patriarchs (including Adam), placed alternately between the haloed apostles or saints, who also hold books.[3] The theme continues to descend and amplify into the lower half of the fresco, in the way now familiar, with on either side (lower bottom) a much more crowded and mixed concourse of divines, sages, doctors, monks and church dignitaries, also intently reading books, poring, discussing, thinking; and some (not all) standing near to and looking at the altar, lower centre. The name 'Disputà' was invented by scholars following Vasari, it seems, who said that the picture (he was speaking, in point of fact, only of the lower half or human level) showed "un numero infinito di Santi che sotto scrivono la messa, e sopra l'ostia che è sullo altare disputano."[4] 'Disputation' or 'disputà' in the older sense of a formal discussion on a fixed theme (not a debate) the picture may in some sense be. It most certainly is, in general terms and as Dussler says, a triumphant affirmation of the Christian faith.[5] But I would agree with Gombrich that Vasari (reflecting a different, post-tridentine theology, though only fifty years after Raphael)[6] overemphasized the subject of the Eucharist as the theme of the entire painting, so distorting its focus.[7] For what the dramatic central panel reveals to us in its descending, tripartite arrangement (evidently an unusual design),[8] is a descent of celestial *light*—illumination, as I take it, to read and interpret correctly the revealed truths of the Scriptures which are held up prominently everywhere: from the more distant intimations of the Old Testament (these books are shown as darker) to the dazzling full revelations of the New, displayed in the four Gospels elevated by winged *putti* at the centre of the upper level, flooded with light, and forming in fact the visual centre of the whole composition. The presiding figure of Theology on the ceiling points directly down to this vertical triptych (so to speak), which constitutes the unified centre panel. At the top of it, surrounded by vast rays of light (among which shadowy cherubim may be detected), is God presiding (for 'God is light', to use Milton's words). He is wearing a solid triangular halo of gold (seen from the front, it resembles an academic 'square'); he holds a globe in his left hand; and the gesture of his right hand is either one of blessing (conventionally so read) or, conceivably, instruction (perhaps both?). He could be seen, then, partly as *instructing* the whole world represented in the globe. Immediately below him, also in half-figure, is Christ, surrounded by a similar but lesser arc of golden rays, arms flung half up in a gesture of divine self-revelation; and below him again is the Holy Spirit in the form of a dove, set against a smaller gold disc with intense rays of light, which seem to reflect directly onto and brightly illuminate the pages of the Gospels proclaiming the Word which are held up on either side. It is evidently that same Spirit who enlightened the saints and sages of the past, shown in the upper panel, that now also shines onto the Gospels and through their bright light into the lives and minds of the men more extensively depicted in their religious studies surrounding: shines as well onto the Altar and Host. 'Enlightenment', then, descending from the Father manifestly onto and into the Son, and through him via the Spirit illuminating the minds and understanding of men in their reading of Scripture to ascertain the faith: that is what the picture says to a post-Miltonist, at any rate; and what Milton could easily have carried away from it. For the main thrust of the painting is surely not toward the altar and the Host (which are below the visual centre and not emphasized):

rather, it is on that remarkable descent of light in the middle panel. And this same 'descent' of light (subtracting of course the lower more Catholic part of the panel—its less dramatic component) may have been the *imagine* which Milton mentally retained: to be refashioned in his Book III Invocation, with its stunning and delicate modulations of all the forms, gradations, and meanings of light, from the most ineffable down to the ordinariness of day, and from the external to the inward light given by the Spirit (in Catholic no less than in Protestant doctrine surely: but by which, according to Milton's more personal and Reformation view as expressed in his *Christian Doctrine*, each Protestant believer was duty-bound to 'winnow and sift' Scripture for himself).[9]

That special motif of the descent of light or spiritual enlightenment ('inspiration' in a disciplined sense) was of peculiar importance to Milton. A similar emphasis on 'light' as instruction or intellectual and spiritual illumination to that which we find in 'The Disputà' characterizes Milton's Book I Invocation ("That Shepherd, who first *taught* the chosen Seed..."; "*Instruct* me, for Thou know'st", 8; 18) and is intrinsic to the intellectual undertaking of the 'great argument'. (It is part of a similar *amplificatio* to Raphael's that in this same context Milton brings in the 'historical' figure of the 'teacher' Moses.) In Book III Invocation (lines 1-55) the light motif again begins 'above', with a direct salutation of 'Holy light' in its pristine source (the allusive syntax brings in the Deity without directly invoking him: "*since* God is Light..."); the 'light' then 'descends' to the Son (first only alluded to, then more directly addressed: "dwelt then in *thee*"; "*hear'st thou* rather pure Ethereal stream"); 'descends' again to the first created light which preceded the cosmos (the sequence is the same as described later by Milton in the Creation scenes in Book VII); descends thence to the 'real' Sun ("[I] *feel* thy sovran... vital Lamp"); to *day*light ("find no dawn"), more dramatic for its ordinariness ("human face divine")—the sight of *things* which through Contemplation leads men to God, denied to the poet ("*wisdom* at one entrance quite shut out"); to, at last, from the source of all ("Celestial Light"), that light which can "shine inward" or the light of the Spirit (the same as is dramatized in Raphael's panel), which is able to "the *mind* through all her powers / Irradiate" and inspire to "see and tell / Of things invisible to mortal sight".[10] Every possible gradation of light—divine (in the Father and Son), light in the precreated cosmos, the Sun, daylight, light as illumination (intellectual, prophetic, poetic): all here are differentiated but fused into a truly essential unity.

It is possible to trace in at least three of the Invocations the same pattern of descent of celestial powers or gifts down to the terrestrial and into the human and the personal. In Book I we witness the descent of the generative Spirit into "the vast Abyss" (20-22)—for Milton 'Spirit' here means the Logos—paralleled by the invoked descent of the same Spirit into "th'upright heart and pure" (18), the material temple (1 *Cor.*, VI. 19) of the body and mind. Book III we have remarked upon. In Book VII there is the invoked descent of Urania down into that created Universe over which she presides ("Descend from Heav'n *Urania*"): paralleled by the poet's own solicited cosmic flights, in imagination, from "rapt above the Pole" (the Uranian vantage point) back down to his "Native Element", "Standing on Earth" (16, 23). Book IX (perhaps because it is prelude to the tragedy-encapsulated-within-the-epic) *declines* at first to invoke any celestial presences, with its abrupt "No more of talk..." and its more matter-of-fact discussion of the Christian epic. Nonetheless a personal counterpart of the 'celestial descent' returns as oblique motif in the hoped-for (rather than invoked) 'descent' of poetic powers, "unimplor'd"—an "answerable stile" given by the "Celestial Patroness" as and when she pleases. Yet the element of divine instruction and divine inspiration persists: "*dictates* to me slumbring, or *inspires*" (23).

Although the Raphael vault may have begun to give us some insight into the matter, it is sometimes quite difficult to see just why or in what way exactly the four Invocations hover between actual prayer or adjuration, and more conventional epic dedication or acknowledgement of a generic Muse: or why within each Invocation the personae or identities addressed should continually waver between celestial-divine and poetico-mythic, or, apparently, even shift between different aspects or persons of the divine Being. This is the aspect of the Invocations which has, I suppose, caused most trouble to scholars. It might have been easier to understand had Milton been content to address only one distinct persona at a time, one in each of the Invocations: for example, the Heavenly Muse in Book I, Father/Son as light in Book III, Urania as cosmic-epic Muse in Book VII. But the sequences are conspicuously not of that simple kind. We have instead in each proem a constant modulation of presences, accompanied by a kind of syntactical slithering—changes sometimes abrupt, sometimes imperceptibly slipping back and forth between several or all of the various identities called upon (although I think we can say that all infer in some manner forms of the divine Wisdom). So in Book I we pass from classical epic adjuration "Sing Heav'nly Muse", with a sharp shift to direct prayer to the Muse as Spirit, in its *instructive* rôle, then to its *creative* agency (in the Dove-figure which for Milton equals the Son): "And *chiefly Thou O Spirit*, that dost preferr... th'upright heart... / ... *Thou from the first / Wast present*...". 'Spirit' is not however entirely distinct from the earlier address to the heavenly 'Muse'—since at first the heavenly muse who *sang* also *inspired* Moses; and "*chiefly* Thou" is a bit ambiguous, as if the second aspect addressed were somehow despite the shift of syntax still a part of the first. And finally we close (not having failed to glance at Old Testament prophecy) with the assertion of eternal Providence and (even if circuitously arrived at) 'the ways of *God*' himself—Providence. The descent in Book III need not be dwelt on further—its remarkable modulations in theme being equalled only by its extraordinary syntax, which contrives to take in in its circling 'descent' not only prophetic light, inspiration of "prophets old", but, simultaneously and indistinguishably, past and present inspired poets: Homer, Milton himself, and (allusively) Orpheus (17). (Orpheus is an important recurring motif in the Invocations: see also VII. 32-38.) We may note again the syntactical tact: all forms of light are directly addressed as *thee*, save the Father, who is included obliquely—"*since* God is Light". This is not a direct prayer to the Father, although it presently may become one to the Son as Logos. The recurring 'thee' communicates some degree of co-identity between all the forms and manifestations of light, higher and lower; from which unity at the last cannot be excepted the fountain of all—the grammar which before seemed to have slipped past God now is seen to have affirmed: "since God *is* Light". And similarly in Book VII, with its apparently new identity introduced or introduced more firmly by name, *Urania*: only to leave us unsure whether under the meaning (not the *name* only, so confusingly taken back again, denied to us) may not be embraced not simply the cosmic deity with her multiple acquired associations, for example of contemplation; or, as well, the traditional Christian epic Muse; but co-equally, some sort of direct aspect of the divine Eternal Wisdom, to whom Urania is Sister (*pre-created* Wisdom this is: "Before the Hills appeerd", 8); while "*in presence of* th'Almightie Father" (11) offers a hint we must draw from as best we can. Book IX Invocation is different, as I have said: more disillusioned as well as less heroic ('more heroic', in new terms). Still, familiar motifs circle back—the Muse, 'celestial patroness' (*not* now 'goddess'—the Greek gods are discredited in line 19). Still, Poetry, as one form of divine inspiration, never ceases to be felt as a divine presence throughout all four Invocations.

Despite all that is so uncertain about these passages, one thing stands out certainly: so much elusiveness and so many ambivalences and multivalencies can only be deliberate—a four times repeated technique which threads together these various Invocations as much as do their reiterated 'descents' and recycled motifs and recurring and overlapping personae. And at this point it is time to draw the argument back once again to Raphael's Stanza. Perhaps it offers one of its most important analogies to *Paradise Lost* in respect most particularly of these *horizontal* dynamics (as well as the vertical dynamic spoken of before)—a movement working across the poem and uniting all the parts of it through the intimately unified personae of the Invocations. On the Stanza vault meanings pass from one sister *imagine* into the next with ease and fluidity, signifying unity-in-diversity, a 'concordance' of knowledges or wisdoms all 'reconciled' in the divine, orchestrating (as Gombrich says) the idea of all knowledges as in some way parts of the same gift from on high. Similarly with the presences appearing, disappearing, reappearing, merging into one another in the poem's four Invocations: the several self-reflecting identities, cognate, complex: Heavenly Muse-Spirit; Holy Light-Father-Son-and-Spirit as inspiration; Urania-Eternal Wisdom-goddess; celestial Patroness. All would appear to be forms of the divine Wisdom whose fountain who shall tell; on which and from whom human wisdoms depend and descend as gifts of the Spirit; and which is reflected in all forms of human wisdom, instructed, poetic, prophetic; in the wisdom to be gained through contemplation of the created and ordered universe; in the inward light which for Milton flows down not exactly from Theology (doctrine) but more directly from the light which is the Father and Son, sometimes via the Spirit. (This last being Milton's personal and protestant refashioning, perhaps, of the message of the third Raphael *imagine*, 'Theology', into that to him more congenial representation of 'light' embodied in the Father, Son and Spirit on the triptych.)

Might it be said, therefore, that Milton seems to have undertaken a not dissimilar kind of intellectual and artistic synthesis on the 'ceiling' of his poem, its four heads or Invocations with their own celestial *imagini* (and vis-à-vis the poem's four narrative 'walls', its main fabric), to that Raphael achieved on the Stanza vault with its interlaced celestial images and their specific connectedness with the wall frescoes below? What Raphael accomplishes with images whose associations seemingly never can be frozen and which continually pass into each other, Milton achieves through a continual modulation of personae invoked or alluded to, coupled with similar associated iconographical motifs similarly descending or opening out into the human concerns of the poet and the poem; and through the exploitation of a grammar and syntax themselves almost numinous—whose meanings like those of Raphael's *imagini* cannot be frozen.

It might spoil what I hope has been a useful analogy to pursue the more general kinds of correspondences that have been traced in the present chapter, too far into the question of indebtedness. It is tempting, for example, to posit that Raphael has a 'Justice' *tondo* and wall, and also a Theology, a Philosophy and a Poetry: and that Milton does too, in the first, third, seventh and ninth Invocations respectively ('Man's first disobedience' and 'eternal Justice'; 'Holy light'; 'Urania-Eternal wisdom'; and the discussion of poetry in Book IX). If we were inclined to pursue such a train of thought, we might find quite a number of other features to support it: such as the observation that Raphael systematically pairs Greek with Hebrew-Christian motifs everywhere in his compositions, in the paired ceiling rectangles, the paired inscriptions, the mixture of classical with Christian figures on the walls; and that Milton also continually does so in the Invocations, rather more pointedly than the mere acknowledgement of a Renaissance convention might require (and quite without the kind of devaluation of the ancient—until Book IX at any rate—that sometimes undermines his uses of classical themes elsewhere in *Paradise Lost*). I think that this particular kind of conjuncture of classical with Christian motifs (as, for example, in the Urania/Eternal Wisdom conflation; or in the drawing together of blind Homer, Moses, also dazzled by his vision, and Orpheus) must presuppose an already Christianized (allegorized) understanding of the classical in both artists. Certainly the conjunction of certain motifs in the context of the Invocations or associated passages seems to fall into place after 'reading' Raphael: Milton's Elijah near Contemplation of the visible cosmos and not far from Urania, and like her 'rapt above the Pole'; Orpheus, twice put into company with the celestial presences and the heavenly Muse. (Orpheus, as I said earlier, in 'poetic theology' could mean the glorified and sacrificed poet-priest, torn and transfigured: a potent myth with something of the same valency as Marsyas-Apollo,[11] but perhaps less ambiguous and more readily recognizable as a pagan-Christian 'type', one into which Milton could more readily pour his own experience, reading himself into the quasi-Christian story in the protestant manner.) Yet in the end, repeated glimpses of systematic programme seem to melt away in Milton's Invocations. Where Raphael's vault works from systematic correspondences and multiplicities brought into a dazzling unity, the unity hinted at by the fragmented personae and fleetingly conjoined motifs in Milton's Invocations is such as finally to elude definition. We must look to Milton's theology for some explanation, and to his personal understanding of Inspiration and its relationship to other forms of knowledge and to poetry.

CHAPTER V

Milton's Theology of the Spirit

If Milton did make use of the Raphael Stanza, or at least of the kind of thinking represented in its programme, it was not without conscious and careful collation with his own theology. Milton can 'orchestrate' meanings as between the various divine or semi-divine presences in his Invocations, or conflate Muse-Urania-Spirit and more ineffable identities, because (I suggest) such a composite view as was presented through the linked *imagini* on the Stanza vault accorded closely with his own understanding of 'Spirit' and the diverse uses of that word in Scripture.[1] Although in the *Christian Doctrine* Milton notes that Scripture says very little in express terms concerning the Spirit; is silent about his origin and nature; and Milton himself expresses doubts as to the co-essentiality, co-equality, or separate nature of this aspect of the divinity (the Spirit while "numerically distinct" and although a "person" is nevertheless not a separate "personality", certainly "is" not the same as God (is not "essentially one" with Him), and always is spoken of as "subservient" or "far inferior" to both God and the Son), Milton nevertheless finds a good deal to say about this equivocal entity. His remarks taken together present in its own way a coherent theological view and an interesting artistic possibility. Milton notes that in the Bible the word 'Spirit' has many uses—ranging in reference from God the Father himself, to the Son (also [Christ as] the Father's "power and virtue"), to the "human mind". It can also at times mean "that impulse or voice of God by which the prophets were inspired"; "that light of truth... wherewith God enlightens and leads his people"; and "spiritual gifts conferred by God on individuals". (Given Milton's view of poetry, such 'gifts' must include the power of poetic inspiration, for him so closely related to prophetic power.[2]) "More particularly", says Milton, 'spirit' "implies that light which was shed on Christ himself". In this context Christ is seen as sharing (but in greater degree) in that same "light of truth" which shone or shines on lesser men: he is the specially favoured recipient of the gift of the Spirit, emanating from or "conferred by God" on individuals. Also, "the Spirit signifies a divine impulse, or light, or voice, or word, transmitted from above either through Christ...

or by some other channel". In this context the "Scriptural expressions themselves", Milton says, do not well "distinguish the Son from the Holy Spirit". Again, although we are not to *pray* to him as if he were a distinct Person, the Spirit may still be "*addressed*" in a way that is "not so much an invocation as a benediction": that is, "not addressed as a person, but sought as a gift".[3] Sought from whom then, or via what "channel", or by what form of words, remains pretty well undefined: resolutely so, one might say.

All of the above senses and all of their ambiguities are latent or explicitly rendered in the careful wordings of Milton's four Invocations. We may note how well the language and distinctions (or lack of them) in the *Christian Doctrine* accord with Milton's wordings and evident inventions in the Invocations. We find in the latter 'Spirit' meaning variously the Father; Christ as Word; as generative power ("the virtue and power of the Father"); gifts conferred on individuals; *light* (especially); the "light of truth"; a "divine impulse, or light, or voice, or word", which may come through but not necessarily only through the agency of the Spirit (we recall Milton "following" the "*Voice* divine" of his Muse). We find that the Spirit may be sought as a gift although not invoked as a Person (contrast the uncertain tone of "And *chiefly* Thou O Spirit... / Instruct me", I. 17, 19, which may be prayer, implying evidently an address to the Son or Father under the term 'Spirit'—or else it is that 'form of benediction' noted above which represents an 'address' to but not an 'invoking' of the Spirit—with the quite different tone—unmistakeably solicitation of a *gift*—to his Muse: "*deignes... unimplor'd*", IX. 20-21; "if all be mine, / Not hers...", 46-47). And that the Spirit is never a separate person but in some way a channel for God's gifts or *wisdom* ("for thou *know'st*"); that he is not well distinguished from the Son (in *Paradise Lost* there is that numinous confusion or conflation between Spirit, illumination, Light, and Logos); that the 'Spirit' *is* in fact the sum of all those forms of illumination or inspiration by whom or which the divine "impulse, or voice, or light or word" reflects into the human mind, understanding and powers ("the mind through *all her powers* / Irradiate[s]"). Phrase after phrase from the Invocations becomes recognizable in the light of the *Christian Doctrine* passages. The "divine impulse, or light, or voice, or word" are all best understood as parts of the divine efficacy or Wisdom: if not always of the essence of the Deity, at least all alike transmitted "from above", either through Christ or "some other channel"—as, variously, in the descent of light in Book III; or in the voice divine of Urania leading the poet in Book I; or the *word* which makes the unformed Matter (and poetic material) "pregnant"; or whatever other form (including the poetic voice). In short, Milton in the Invocations plays on *all* the meanings of 'spirit' in order to make the theological point that these usages are both various and interrelated. The vagueness and shifting meanings of 'spirit' as defined in the *Christian Doctrine* are deliberately exploited by him, through the fluid syntax and shifting names and personae, emphasized as different yet not completely distinguishable from each other. The different senses blur and merge, fusing apparent distinctions into a felt unity: just as elsewhere in *Paradise Lost* syntax and presentation blur and fuse the identities (initially presented as separate) of Father and Son, Judge and Intercessor (the confused or fused persons of Son and Father in the Judgement Scene in Book X being a salient example). Perhaps in the end it is the simple "light of truth" that best explains to our modern understandings all these different interconnected meanings. The difficult conceptual point for a modern reader to take in is that diverse though all the senses of 'spirit' may seem (or personae as represented in the 'Invocations'), they all in some way reflect facets of that same truth which is felt to be first in God, and in various ways subsequently differentiated or emanating from him. All are *differing* aspects of truth (or Knowledge or Wisdom); but all *merge* in and *emerge* from a common source. Hence it is conceptually appropriate that in the proems invocations, prayers, solications, rhetorical addresses, allusions or musings should modulate, shift, return. The perspective may alter as to the different aspects of the divine intended, or shift from divine to human. But truth, and light, prophetic or poetic inspiration, knowledge and understanding do not in their essence change: they are the same, even if different men receive them in different measure or in different ways or by different means. The light which "is" God contains that which shines on and graces the Son ("dwelt then in thee"); also (via the Son or the Spirit or other channel) descends into men. So with all forms of truth and wisdom: whether that acquired through Contemplation (which is in men a smaller reflection of the divine *meraviglia*); or learned through 'instruction' by the Spirit (in the reading of Scripture); or imparted by the Christian Muse ('celestial song' being equally as 'pleasing' to God as 'wisdom'). Like the different lights of a prism, all these lights or meanings shine out at different times in the enigmatic unities of the Invocations. In them, Milton inflects his theology of the Spirit according to his own particular understanding—not wholly conventional even in protestant terms. Yet even as we reflect on this question, it is not clear how much difference may really exist (or need to be seen to exist) between the modulating personae of Milton's Invocations and Raphael's celestial *imagini*, the interlinked manifestations of Wisdom wheeling around and resolving in their divine centre—whether broadly speaking each artist was not making use of some of the largest enduring Christian *topoi*. Reading Milton's Invocations, with their distinctive yet indistinct personae, flanked by so many concrete human figures past and present and concrete visual details, we might imagine ourselves, as nearly as is possible in a different medium, to be regarding Raphael's mysteriously linked celestial presences above their Parnassian or other settings. For such *concetti* surely represented conceptions which every Renaissance and Christian artist and scholar felt himself invited to reflect upon, add to, reinterpret and reformulate for himself.

I think it therefore entirely natural that Milton might have turned to Raphael's Stanza to help him structure and orient the Invocations, to find an iconography to embody the intellectual conceptions he needed to present in the four 'heads' to the poem, to interrelate their figures and orchestrate them into the poem at large. Only because his own understanding of the theology of the 'Spirit' accorded so closely with the *spirit* of Raphael's celestial *imagini* could, I suppose, Milton feel free to make such a use, if he did. For if his own theology gave him the intellectual content of the Invocations, I believe that the Stanza vault and its relationships with its walls may have given him the general design and the iconographic means of its poetic amplification.

CHAPTER VI

The Literary Urania

A more mundane coda must follow, as briefly as is possible: since to embark on such a matter is to open up a whole new and extensive area of study. That is, the question of the literary Urania, the well-known Muse of European cosmological-epic and Christian-epic tradition stretching back through Du Bartas to (though this is not so generally known) at least Raphael's time. The question of course arises how much in the Invocations Milton might have derived from the literature of the French or English Du Bartas or other epic poets, rather than from traditions of visual iconography such as Raphael's. There is no straightforward answer to that question: since the histories of the literary predecessors of *Paradise Lost* are so mutually entangled and their interconnectedness with visual iconography of the fifteenth and sixteenth centuries so difficult to determine. But I shall try to glance back through some European Christian epic and associated long cosmic or Creation poems of pre-1600 (leaving out the somewhat uninspired pre-Miltonic English epic).

Tasso, the nearest to Milton in time, offers an obvious parallel to Milton's Muse in the *Gerusalemme liberata*'s opening Invocation. His Muse is there called upon (fleetingly yet with a certain visual evocativeness) as a "heavenly muse", crowned not "with fading baies" nor near "th'Heliconian spring" but sitting instead in Heaven "crownd with stars immortal raies".[1] This address to a Muse heavenly, poetic and cosmic ('stars' rays' indicate the last), though she appears only once in the poem, might suggest a diluted recollection of the Raphael *imagine* (or some similar). But Tasso plays down this Muse in favour of subsequent direct descriptions of or prayers to the Father. Perhaps significantly, he gives her no name.[2] However, a gap of under ten years between Du Bartas' "L'Uranie" (1574) and the *Première Sepmaine* (1578)[3] and Tasso's epic (1581-82) makes some connection with Du Bartas (perhaps here mere acknowledgement) and his well-known poems not unlikely. Much more relevant to Milton is Tasso's expanded undertaking of a Christian Creation poem (which by 1592 he would have had time to develop from the Bartasian model) in the *sette giornati* of his *Il Mondo Creato*, in which all invocatory address or allusion is firmly directed not to any Muse but specifically as prayer to the Father or to Him, the Son and the Spirit—most memorably in the opening of the First Day, with its close thematic and linguistic anticipations of *Paradise Lost*, Invocation III, and its so similar prayer for a *descent* of light from Father-Son-Spirit into the poet ("in me discendi"): light there to be received as instruction and poetic inspiration.[4] There is nothing in all of Du Bartas so close in feeling to Milton, or to match the poetic sensitivity and delicacy of theological-linguistic inflection, as this passage from the *Mondo Creato*, which Milton entirely recaptured in Book III. Yet this extraordinary, mystical passage, with its rarefied and spiritualized diction, has intermixed none of the concrete particularities concerning light nor concrete details from the Parnassian context which in Milton make us think also of Raphael.

The Bartasian connections of *Paradise Lost*, from both French and English versions, are more extensive yet in many ways less intrinsic than are the poem's connections with Tasso. (And, as with the Tasso-Fairfax-Milton triangle, the whole matter of the Du Bartas-Sylvester-Milton association is much complicated by the fact that Milton sometimes borrows small striking verbal phrasings from the translations or particular details added by the two Elizabethans, while in spirit and dignity of feeling and diction remaining much closer to the French and Italian originals, which he also knew and borrowed from or adapted freely.) With Merritt Hughes[5] one may say that Milton's Muse is much more than the Urania made so popular by Du Bartas and Sylvester. (Perhaps the very fact that Milton casts doubt on the name 'Urania' indicates that he, while making use of the Bartasian tradition, wishes to indicat5 that his muse is not the same as Du Bartas'.) Milton's muse is more elusive too, and the Invocations altogether more enigmatic and complex than Du Bartas' six proems, which are really little more than prefaces, one preceding each of the first six 'Days'. Despite their many extended general resemblances to *Paradise Lost*, we might well conclude that it is the differences which stand out more.

To begin with, Du Bartas in most cases clearly divides his 'Invocations' in an almost mechanical way into two parts, distinguishing regularly between actual prayers to the Deity, who is invoked in all his varied capacities as Creator, Inspirer of Learning and Wisdom, Ruler, Judge, Guide ("O Father", "eternall Father", "Almightie Father", Days I, V and VI; "Architect", Days I and VII; "O King", Day III; "Great Soveraigne of the Seas", Day VI),[6] and rhetorical addresses to the Muse. The Muse, when she appears (the address to her usually following one to the Father), is clearly differentiated and secondary: no numinousness. She is either exhorted or more often described in the course of her cosmic or earthly journies. Something of a celestial acrobat, she "soared high", or is seen "flagging lowly by the ground".[7] She retains very conspicuously and unambiguously her cosmic rôle "among the glist'ring Circles of the Skye": although somehow there has been superadded a capacity to descend into and tell the wonders of the lower orders of Nature.[8] But never does she rise into Milton's 'Heaven of Heavens' or show any family relationship with Wisdom, God, or the Spirit. (It is interesting that Du Bartas, although by and large keeping clear the distinction between 'Father' and 'Muse', himself in the French does use the word "Esprit" for Muse, and also, perhaps with intended ambivalence, "mon esprit":[9] but Sylvester prefers when he can to translate 'Muse'.[10]) Their Urania's role is thus clearly defined and restricted: it is not this Muse/Spirit who (in some fashion linked with God) is "Cleare Source of Learning, soule of th'Universe",[11] or communicates the gifts of the Spirit. She is merely, as persona of the poet and epitome of his literary energy, the 'she' who relates and poetically elevates. The constant references to her as 'divine' therefore concern her subject rather than her person or spiritual role.

While clearly Milton as a Protestant may have taken something from the double personae and self-conscious differentiation between doctrine or prayer and poetical rhetoric in Du Bartas' Invocations, one cannot but wonder why he should then have taken such evident pains partly to blur back again those very plain distinctions between Father and Muse, prayer and mere rhetorical *invocatio*, so carefully sustained by his two Protestant predecessors. The mysteriously fluctuating and merging personae and addresses of his own proems have ultimately little in common with Du Bartas'. Nor is there anything in the *Sepmaine* Invocations at all resembling the closely interwoven thematic textures and complicated overlappings of the Miltonic Invocations. Each of the first six Bartasian Invocations in a rather practical way indicates material to follow (courtesy of the Muse): a prayer appropriately often preceding. Again this offers little resemblance to the intricate four-pillared structure of Milton's proems (all developing their linked-yet-different aspects of divine Wisdom, illumination or instruction), which makes of each Invocation a distinct yet parallel 'descent' from the celestial down into the human, and by extension into the expanded narration of each main section of *Paradise Lost.* Not only are Milton's Invocations and personae more complex and more structured, but there is a great difference between a *preface* and a *conceit* or *imagine*. Whatever Milton assimilated from Du Bartas (and one can see that in simple ways he derived quite a lot), something much more complex has been superadded or intervened: something more, even, than the numinous impact of Tasso's Creation poem can explain.

This is not to say that many memorable phrases or thoughts from the *Sepmaine* (also from Sylvester's *Divine Weekes*) did not spark off important echoes in *Paradise Lost*. Apart from the prayerful elements in the Bartasian Invocations, which clearly influenced Milton's, there is, for example, the remarkable correspondence to Milton's wish for an "answerable style" in Du Bartas' own hope "that it [his style] may have / Some correspondence to a Theame so grave" and his prayer "Oh furnish me with an unvulgar style."[12] There is also a notable passage in Day IV (which like the opening of Day I conjoins an allusion to Elijah and his chariot of fire); here I quote:

> Pure Spirit, that rapt'st above the Firmest Spheare,
> In fierie Coach, thy faithfull Messenger,
> Who smiting *Jordan* with his pleighted Cloake,
> Did yerst devide the Waters with the stroake:
> O take me up; that farre from Earth, I may
> From Spheare to Spheare, see th'azure Heav'ns *To Day*.
> Bee thou my Coach-man, and now Cheeke by Joule
> With *Phoebus* Chariot let my Chariot roule;
> Drive on my Coach by *Mars* his flaming Coach;
> *Saturne* and *Luna* let my wheeles approach:
> That having learn'd of their Fire-breathing Horses,
> Their course, their light, their labour, and their forces,
> My Muse may sing in sacred Eloquence,
> To vertues Friends, their vertuous Excellence:
> And with the Load-stone of my conquering Verse,
> Above the Poles attract the most perverse.
> And you faire learned soules, you spirits divine,
> To whom the Heav'ns so nimble quils assigne,
> As well to mount, as skilfully to limne
> The various motion of their Tapers trimme;
> Lend me your hand; lift me above *Pernassus*;
> With your loud *Trebles* helpe my lowly *Bassus*:
> . . . .
> But, if thy wits thirst rather seeke these things,
> In *Greekish* cesternes then in *Hebrew* springs...

Who could suppose that Milton's 'rapt above the Pole' did not glance at this passage?[13] (As well, of course, the Miltonic preference for "Sion's hill", *PL*, I. 10, a distinction to which Milton, like Du Bartas, constantly returns.) But the remarkable clarity of visual detail in this Bartasian (or Sylvestrian) passage, and especially the casual reference to being lifted above a Parnassus (as if everyone would recognize the allusion) might themselves suggest an iconographical source such as the Raphael 'Parnassus' and 'Poetry' (or some similar among the numerous sixteenth-century models). To me it seems that the combination of Sphere(s), rapture, the Pole, and 'Pernassus' could well convey some generalized recollection of the Raphael configuration in the Stanza. Is it the case then that Milton is remembering Du Bartas: or that both of them are remembering the same famous painting, or some similar, or a number of models—Milton acknowledging the Bartasian imitation *en passant* but (characteristically) going back to a more major original source?

Here the line of literary-iconographical descent becomes surprisingly complex. For it was not Du Bartas who invented the cosmic-poetic Muse he so confidently called Urania: but (if even he was the first) the much earlier Latin poet J. J. Pontanus (Pontano), an almost exact contemporary of Raphael. Pontanus wrote at least two narrative cosmological poems (we could almost call them Creation poems): one long, the other longer still, the one actually entitled "Urania",[14] but both containing opening or concluding perorations citing that goddess as the presiding Muse of the Heavens and of the poetic undertaking (in spirit a praise of the Creation, in detail a description of the cosmos). Although Pontanus' images are secular and to do with the pagan gods, they belong to that earlier stage of Renaissance humanism which could deploy such images with an almost total moral didacticism and a quasi-Christian feeling behind the pagan pantheon.[15] It cannot be accidental that *both* Du Bartas and Milton echo or paraphrase from the very opening of Pontanus' early poem two lines which must have been famous:

> *Dic Dea, quae nomen coelo deducis* ab ipso
> *Uranie, dic Musa* Jovis clarissima proles[16]

So Du Bartas, in his earlier poem *also called* "L'Uranie": she now however having become the 'sacred Muse', later the inspirer of the *Première Sepmaine*:

> Ainsi m' admonestoit la Muse, *qui on appelle*
> *Du nom du ciel vouté.*[17]

(There is a double allusion here, of course: first to the Greek root of the Muse's name [*Ourania* = Heaven/sky]; second, to the Pontanus.) So Milton, more pointedly, also: recollecting, acknowledging, *correcting*, returning to sources with the enlarged historical perspective which is cognizant of multiple derivations (but including perhaps a more direct visual memory of the Raphael images and a truer awareness of their inner meaning)—Milton reformulating once again the many times reformulated images:

> Descend from Heav'n *Urania, by that name*
> *If rightly thou art calld*, . . . for thou
> Nor of the Muses nine, nor on the top
> Of old *Olympus* dwellst, but *Heav'nlie borne*
> . . . still govern thou my Song,
> *Urania* . . . .
> *Say Goddess*, what ensu'd when *Raphael* . . .
> (VII. 1-40)

It seems significant that it should be here, the only place in *Paradise Lost* where Milton names his Muse, naming her *twice*, in wordings which unmistakeably echo Pontanus (even to the same words being placed in the same positions in lines 30 and 40),[18] that Milton departs from the traditional name in search of a more ineffable *meaning*, passing beyond the conventional Muse of Christian epic popularized by Du Bartas though deriving more likely from Pontanus (however by now fully Christianized)—passing beyond, that is, a literary Muse who was a simple conflation of cosmological and poetic virtù, of 'celestial' origin perhaps and, later, sacred avocation, but not in herself of any divine essence or potency.

Where did that particular conflation still so confidently employed by Du Bartas nearly a century after Pontanus emanate from? Was there in Du Bartas' mind both a recollection of Pontanus with as well some confused recollection of Raphael's two linked figures of 'Urania' and Poetry? Or possibly of these with several other such visual and iconographical representations? Did the famous Pontanus, great poet and humanist, himself inspire,[19] or someone else of the scholarly circle surrounding Raphael help to direct, the much more complicated visual iconography of Raphael's vault? Did Raphael himself reflect and enlarge on one or more earlier, simpler visual images?[20] How many later visual representations in the same tradition—emblems, for example, or distorted visual renderings of Raphael himself (such as are evident in many subsequent engravings of the Stanza)—stand between Pontanus and Raphael on the one hand, and Du Bartas and Milton on the other? It is not possible to suggest definite answers to all of these questions. But it must have been the case that literary and visual iconographical traditions on such themes were closely interacting over the course of a century and a half or more, and so interwined as to be almost inseparable for any present day analysis.[21] It is evident to this reader, at any rate, that Du Bartas was indulging in a poetic euphemism as to the sources of his inspiration, and that it came from something rather more concrete than a dream. For the earlier "L'Uranie" which contains the echo of Pontanus above has a revealing preface, a separate little poem inserted into the later editions, describing an alleged dream-vision of the poet, a vision of his 'Uranie'. I give part of this below:

Or, tandis qu'inconstant je ne me puis resoudre,
Deça, delà, poussé d'un vent ambitieus,
Une sainte beauté se presente à mes yeux,
Fille, comme je croi, du grand Dieu lance-foudre.

Sa face est angelique, angelique son geste;
Son discours tout divin, et tout parfait son cors;
Et sa bouche à neuf vois imite en ses accors
Le son harmonieus de la dance celeste.

Son chef est honoré d'une riche corone
Faite à set plis glissans d'un divers mouvement—
Sur chacun de ses plis se tourne obliquement
Je ne sçai quel rondeau, qui sur nos chefs raione.

Le premier est de plom, et d'etain le deusieme,
Le troisieme d'acier, le quart d'or jaunissant,
Le quint est composé d'electre palissant,
Le suivant de mercure, et d'argent le settieme.

Son cors et affublé d'une mante azurée,
Semée haut et bas d'un milion de feus
Qui d'un bel art sans art, distinctement confus,
Decorent de leur rais cete beaute sacrée.

Ici luit le grand char, ici flambe la lyre,
Ici la poussiniere, ici les clers bessons;
Ici le trebuchet, ici les deus poissons,
Et mile autres brandons que je ne puis decrire.

—Je suis (dit-elle alors) cete docte Uraine
Qui sur les gons astrés transporte les humains,
Faisant voir à leurs yeux et toucher à leurs mains
Ce que la cour celeste et contemple et manie.

Je quinte-essence l'ame et fai que le poete,
Se surmontant soi-mesme, enfonce un haut discours
Qui, divin, par l'oreille atire les plus sours,
Anime les rochers et les fleuves arrete.

Agreable est le son de mes doctes germaines;
Mais leur gosier, qui peut terre et ciel enchanter,
Ne me cede pas moins en l'art de bien chanter
Qu'au rossignol l'oison, les pies au serenes.

65a Pren-moi donques pour guide, eleve au ciel ton aile!
Salluste, chante-moy du Tout-puissant l'honeur,
Et remontant le lut du Josséan soneur,
Courageus, brosse apres la corone eternele!
14-20 A.B: Et s'il a quelque bien, tant peu soit precieus,
Par differentes mains il l'a receu des cieus;
Mais Dieu seul nous aprend les chansons delphienes.[22]

The description is such as could not but have derived from detailed reminiscences of one or more visual representations of the subject: paintings in the first instance, one might suppose, or engravings of them from books; or earlier emblems, such as those in the Tarocchi series—the great Ripa collection being not yet printed by the time of Du Bartas' poem. The complicated crown of various metals worn by Du Bartas' Uranie has certainly nothing to do with Raphael. But the characteristic Urania-zodiacal signs are clearly in evidence ("les clers bessons", "les deus poissons"). And much else in the picture might be a recollection of Raphael's 'Urania' figure—even if filtered through later iconographical models—most hauntingly her blue cloak sown all over with innumerable stars, "distinctement confus", and the heavenly beauty of her figure and pose ("sa face... angelique, angelique son geste")—impressions which no emblem could convey. Even here, if it *is* Raphael remembered, we have traces of further visual conflations: not only of a 'Urania' with a 'Poetry' but, here, a Poetry who has a "grand char" (not in the Stanza figure) as well as a "lyre" (like that of 'Poetry' in 'The Parnassus'). Yet oddly, this "*docte* Urane" in the earlier poem seems for just a moment to be a bit closer to the celestial *imagini* of the Raphael Stanza than does the later cosmic acrobat of the *Sepmaine*: "*Fille*, comme je croi, *du grand Dieu* lance-foudre". Milton too saw Urania-Poetry as something akin to a daughter of God. The humbler Protestant poet, less flexible, less subtle in his poetic projection of doctrine, and less rich in his sense of meaningful continuities, felt constrained to retract. Thus his final line: "*Mais Dieu seul nous aprend les chansons delphienes*". The Urania whom Du Bartas evoked in his later better known work represents a diminishing of the intellectual content and context of the original Raphael *concetti*: contexts which, it would seem, Milton with a larger perspective felt able to restore. Who in any case—having once seen them—could ever have failed to remember and retain implanted on the inward eye especially that most ravishing of the Stanza's *imagini*: the figure of 'Urania' leaning forward in her absorbed contemplation of the universe, seemingly already part way down from the heavens, as if ready at any moment to descend, although still placed next to Wisdom and also to divine Poetry: the latter seated high above the Parnassus, her great wings extended as if poised to take flight into those infinite distances upon which her eyes seem fixed? So perfectly captured in Milton's own image-conceit of the 'descent from Heaven' of Urania, coupled with the poet's flight into the heaven of heavens high above the Parnassian hill on her wing.

APPENDIX I: 'UT PICTURA POESIS'

The notion of *ut pictura poesis* was a commonplace, and one which could be made to work in either direction. With respect to painting, the correlation often specifically implied an 'invention' equivalent to that kind of abstract 'idea' which would normally be conveyed by poetry (often, allegorical poetry). Although the precise senses of 'invention' or 'idea' could vary (the words sometimes meant merely 'design' or aesthetic conception), the following well-known contemporary passages all convey primarily the former or 'conceptual' sense.

L. B. Alberti, *De Pictura* (1435):

> [poets and orators] have many ornaments in common with the painter. Literary men, who are full of information about many subjects, will be of great assistance in preparing the composition of a 'historia', and *the great virtue of this consists primarily in its invention. Indeed, invention is such that even by itself and without pictorial representation it can give pleasure.* [Italics mine.]

From L. B. Alberti, *On Painting and on Sculpture*, Latin texts ed. and transl. by C. Grayson (London, 1972), Bk. III, p. 96 (Lat. text, p. 95).

'Lettera di Raffaello al Castiglione' (1514):

> Ho fatto disegni in più maniere *sopra l'inventione di V.S.*, e sodisfaccio a tutti. . . . [Italics mine.]

From V. Golzio, ed., *Raffaello: nei documenti nelle testimonianze dei contemporanei e nella letteratura del suo secolo* (Città del Vaticano, 1936; corr. ed. 1971), p. 30.

G. Vasari, 'Vita di Raffaello da Urbino' (1550):

> Fece Raffaello in questa storia San Pietro e San Paulo in aria con le spade in mano che vengono a difender la Chiesa: e se bene la storia di Leon III non dice questo, egli nondimeno per capriccio suo volse figurarla forse così, *come interviene molte volte che così le pitture come le poesie vanno vagando* per ornamento dell'opera, non si discostando però *per modo non conveniente dal primo intendimento.* [Italics mine.]

From *Le Vite de' più eccellenti pittori, scultori e architettori*, ed. R. Bettarini, Vol. IV (Florence, 1976), p. 183.

[A. Caro] A M. Giòrgio Vasari Dipintore, a Firenze (1548):

> ... che ancora de l'inventione mi rimetto a voi, ricordandomi d'*un' altra somiglianza, che la poesia hà con la pittura*, et di più, che voi siete *cosi poeta come pittore*, et *che ne l'una et ne l'altra* con più affettione et con più studio *s'esprimono i concetti et le idee sue proprie che d'altrui.* [Italics mine.]

Letter CXII, from *Der literarische Nachlass Giorgio Vasaris*, ed. K. Frey (Munich, 1923), I, p. 220; also transl. by E. Gombrich, in *The Heritage of Appelles: Studies in the Art of the Renaissance* (Oxford, 1976), pp. 124-25.

Alberti praises 'invention' as the greatest merit in painting and as a literary conception which can exist even without the painting. Raphael speaks of an antecedent 'invention' (another's) which he has tried to execute in a painting. Vasari asserts the right of the painter as of the poet to defy history or depart from his original story in order further to embellish his work. And Caro declares that poetry and painting resemble each other, the more so in that each best expresses the 'conceits' or 'ideas' of the painter or another person. Over a century, the assumptions that paintings like poems have something to 'say', something literary and conceptual and beyond the illustrative, evidently has altered not at all.

APPENDIX II: THE MILTONIC URANIA

There has been a long tradition of critical uncertainty on this subject. On Urania and the Invocations, see, *inter alia*: E. M. W. Tillyard, *Milton* (London, 1930; rev. ed., 1962), pp. 246-47; L. B. Campbell, *Divine Poetry and Drama in Sixteenth-Century England* (Cambridge and Berkeley, 1959), pp. 75-80 and 97-99, and also "The Christian Muse", *H.L.B.*, VIII (1935), pp. 29-70; M. Kelley, *This Great Argument: A Study of Milton's De Doctrina Christiana as a Gloss upon Paradise Lost* (Princeton, 1941; repr. Gloucester, Mass., 1962), pp. 106-18; D. Daiches, "The Opening of 'Paradise Lost'" in *The Living Milton*, ed. F. Kermode (London, 1960), pp. 55-69; and M. Y. Hughes, "Milton and the Symbol of Light", *S.E.L.*, 4 (1964), pp. 1-33. Hughes answers W. B. Hunter's article in the same volume, "Milton's Urania", *S.E.L.*, 4 (1964), pp. 35-42. (See also W. B. Hunter, "The Meaning of 'Holy Light' in *Paradise Lost* III", *M.L.N.*, LXXIV, 1959, pp. 589-92.) Hunter argues connections via Spenser's "Hymne to Heavenlie Beauty" with the Neoplatonic-Christian traditions of 'Sapience', and argues that in 'Light' Milton is addressing the Logos.

Critics have been divided between those who see a number of different figures 'invoked' in the four Invocations (a procedure which they find difficult) and those who look for a single or one main meaning throughout. Briefly, e.g.: Hughes (p. 20) agrees with Daiches (p. 64) in finding that in Invocation I the stress is on prophetic inspiration ("Wisdom and understanding"). (Daiches' stress in fact is on Bk. VII and on the *various* forms 'inspiration' via the 'Spirit' may take, including the 'creative' or poetic form. He is correct in this, as Milton's *Commonplace Book* entries under 'Poetry' confirm: see chapter 5, n. 2.) In Invocation III, Hunter finds in the images of light evidence of a 'two-stage Logos' (*M.L.N.* article) and in *S.E.L.* (p. 35) attempts to extend this interpretation as valid for all of the Invocations, and specifically to "the only named divinity", Urania, in Book VII. A. Fowler (see chap. 3, n. 3) finds a more consistent Muse (whether in Book III or throughout all four Invocations is not clear) in the "more recent, single Muse" of the Du Bartas poetic tradition (see his note to VII. 1-7). M. Kelley, in contrast (p. 117), believes that Milton is addressing "a personification of various attributes of God the Father", rather than the Holy Spirit as has often been supposed. M. Hughes (p. 20) declines to be drawn into too narrow an identification of Milton's *persona* or *personae* with the Son, arguing that in the light of *The Christian Doctrine*, I. vi (see chapter 5, n. 1) it hardly seems justifiable to insist that Milton "was consciously praying... for the afflation of the Son of God, as something to be distinguished from 'that light [i.e., prophetic inspiration] which was shed on Christ himself' and upon Moses and the prophets". He is also quite firm (p. 13) that "Milton's Urania is not simply the Christianized Muse" of the Du Bartas tradition traced by Lily

Campbell. (Campbell's declaration that Du Bartas introduced a *new* Christian Muse to the Western world was ill-judged; such a Muse was neither new, nor her iconography invented by him.)

Hunter has two interesting perceptions which one wishes he had pursued: the one (p. 37) that the poet is oddly "mixing nationalities by asserting such a close family relationship between a Hebrew and a Greek figure" (in Invocation VII); the other (p. 39) that in Urania's 'Sister' Wisdom, "the poetic use... might be deliberately ambivalent". The first item is, of course, basic to that pairing of Christianized-pagan and Christian iconography consistently employed by both Milton and Raphael; and the deliberate 'poetic ambiguity' of the second suggestion is (as I argue) confirmed by Milton's theology.

Recently J. M. Steadman has summed up the scholarly arguments to date: see 'Urania' entry in *A Milton Encyclopedia*, 9 vols., ed. W. B. Hunter *et al.* (London and Toronto, 1978-83), Vol. 8 (1980), pp. 106-13. Steadman's conclusion is inconclusive: the variety of interpretation is too great to allow resolution of the question. He himself inclines to the view that Milton is "associating his Urania with biblical rather than mythological tradition" (p. 107) and that (in Bk. I) "Taken together, [the] appeals to the Muse and the Spirit are complementary; and in the final analysis they refer to powers or operations of the same 'Spirit of God'" (p. 113).

Earlier, N. Henry arrived at a conclusion both different and related: Milton's Muse *is* linked to myth and rhetoric; and she *is* also a composite personality in Christian as well as literary terms: "In Milton's shifting references" one may discern "a triune fusion" (p. 75) [i.e., "a Christian Muse reflecting three parts of the Godhead", p. 80]; but this is a "rhetorical conceit" and not an explicitly theological one. "Milton has constructed a literary conceit, or literary 'mystery', analogous to a theological one... deliberate and contrived... not inscrutable in terms of the usage of Homer, Lucretius, Virgil, Dante, Tasso, or Spenser, in all of whom the muse seems indefinite, multiple, many-named, somewhat mysterious" (pp. 78-79). See "The Mystery of Milton's Muse," *Renaissance Papers* (1967), pp. 69-83.

It appears to me that scholars have been impeded by their tendency to look either to Scripture and Milton's theology on the one hand, or to classical literary antecedents on the other. It is in the middle ground where both of those meet in the Renaissance, the visual iconography shared by Christian poets and painters alike, where Christianized myth branches into complex *concetti*, that the full answers to the dilemma appear to lie: revealing that Milton's Urania is an extremely complex conception, combining elements from many intellectual and artistic backgrounds, reworked and moulded into his own theology.

APPENDIX III: 15C-17C EMBLEMS

'Masters of the Tarocchi' Series (15C)

These are reproduced in K. Obertuber *et al.*, *Early Italian Engravings from the National Gallery of Art* (Washington, D.C., 1973). Besides the 'Theology' and 'Urania' figures cited in n. 20 to chap. 6, a number of other figures in the 'Apollo and the Muses', 'Liberal Arts', 'Three Cosmic Powers' and 'Firmaments of the Universe' groups of the series also have details showing analogies to the iconography of the Stanza vault. These include:

'Apollo' (Pl. 34, p. 112): shown crowned and robed, seated on a throne, with under his feet a sphere (one half starry).

'Philosophia' (Pl. 42, p. 122): is represented by Minerva ("Since she was regarded as a Goddess of Wisdom, she could serve by extension as a personification of Philosophy": eds., quoting Tervarent). We may cf. Raphael's 'Philosophy' in her connections with Wisdom (divine).

'Poesia' (Pl. 40, p. 120): seated, holds a flute, cup, and also a sphere (the sphere is divided: the upper half is starry, the lower shows the earth). The eds. note that Poetry has been inserted into the normal Quadrivium sequence: we may cf. Raphael's 'Poetry' as a form of learning or wisdom, and the Miltonic Urania's kinship with Wisdom. We may note this early association of Poetry with the heavens; although here she is still earth-bound (seated on the ground). Not so later.

'Cosmico' (Pl. 46, p. 127): or 'Genius of the World'; he carries a similar divided sphere to Poesia's. (Raphael's 'Urania' has been thought to represent the cosmic Universe; the literary Urania sings of both heavens and the earth.)

'Octava spera' (Pls. 63, 64, pp. 154-55): the 'Eighth Sphere', or that of the fixed stars, holds a larger starry sphere which is closer in size to that of the 'Theologia' or Raphael's 'Urania'.

'Primo Mobile' (Pl. 65, p. 156): holds a sphere evidently hollow or empty, yet also apparently solid. Eds.: "The ninth and last of the material spheres.... Crystalline and invisible, it is in direct contact with God." There are visual affinities here to the solid or crystalline spheres associated with Raphael's 'Urania' (or God in the Chigi chapel) and with Milton's Satan (and God) in Bk. III.

It is evident in how many complex ways these earlier figures interrelate with each other, as do Raphael's later figures on the vault, and the Miltonic emblems.

Cesare Ripa, 'Iconologia' (17C)

These are to be found in a number of illustrated editions from 1603 onwards. The descriptions which follow are taken from J. Baudouin's translation, with moralizations, in the Paris edition of 1644, *Iconologie*, facs. series 'The Renaissance and the Gods', No. 29, ed. S. Orgel (New York and London, 1976). However, the illustrations at the end of this study are taken from a later edition of Baudouin (*Iconologie*, Paris, 1677) in the University Library, Cambridge. The text and illustrations of this later edition are identical, but the page numberings differ (in 1677, Part I, pp. 29, 48, 198, 237; Part II, pp. 89, 248: for the pictures as shown facing p. 34).

'Astrologie' (Pt. I, p. 22): a majestic figure, plainly gowned, holding a pair of compasses in one hand, and in the other a starry globe at which she gazes. She has a crown of stars, and extended wings. The gloss (p. 24) tells us that her dress is *blue*, to show that she contemplates the stars and skies; that she is winged, because she lifts the spirit to higher things.

'Theologie' (Pt. I, p. 184): she appears in almost the identical pose and situation to those in the Tarocchi drawing; but the starry globe has an added zodiacal band, the lady's dress is elaborated on, and a lower half has been added to her torso. That is, she still appears to be standing behind and above the starry sphere; but she is also, so to speak, sitting 'side-saddle' *upon* it. Despite the odd distortion, the impression of the original has not been lost.

'Poesie' (Pt. I, p. 152): a figure with a lyre (more like a cello) and flute, crowned with laurel, and clad in a starry mantle. The gloss informs us (p. 158) that her starry robe is in sign of her divinity, since, according to the poets, that art draws its origin from the Sky.

'Uranie' (Pt. II, p. 71): gowned plainly, starry crown, holding an orrery; her compasses are on the ground. The gloss (p. 76) notes that her name comes from the Greek for 'heaven'/'sky'; and she is so named because she raises men to those heights.

'Astrologie' (Pt. II, p. 188): A more complex figure, with starry dress, starry crown, and a jewel (a sun) on her breast. This time she holds a sceptre and has an eagle at her feet. Her starry globe has a band with figures of the zodiac. The gloss (p. 190) says only that all these items indicate that her eyes are constantly fixed upon the stars.

It may be seen that the above figures follow earlier emblems such as the 'Tarocchi' in many details, but become more elaborate. Like the earlier figures, these also overlap, interweave and conflate in increasingly complex ways.

NOTES

NOTES TO CHAPTER I

1 This is the view of Gordon Campbell, who thinks that Parker (see n. 2 below) is mistaken on this point, and that Milton saw Holstenius twice—the first, more formal visit having taken place in October/November 1638.

2 This is well documented—see W. R. Parker, *Milton: a Biography*, 2 vols. (Oxford, 1968), I, pp. 176-77; also J. M. French, n. 4 below; and J. Arthos, *Milton and the Italian Cities* (London, 1968). J. H. Hanford has followed the footsteps of Milton's journey (see "Milton in Italy", *Annuale Mediaevale*, 5, 1964, pp. 49-63). Among other interesting information Hanford gives are included the following: (1) Milton may have had a particularly warm welcome from Holstenius (whose employer and patron was Cardinal F. Barberini, although Holstenius was even then acting informally as Vatican librarian), because of a mutual connection with the bookseller, J. Thomason. (2) The party Milton attended at the Palazzo Barberini (F. Barberini was a poet, scholar, a classicist and patron of the arts) may well have been an historic performance of the comic opera, 'Chi Soffre Spera", for which Bernini provided stage-designs. (3) Another Barberini contact from Rome, Doni, spoke at the Svogliati academy in Florence, when Milton visited it in 1639. Such connections put Milton at the heart of not only the world of Italian poetry and theoretical criticism, but also that of opera and art.

3 This would have been the main Vatican library, and not the Stanza della Segnatura, the subject of the present article. On the history of the latter, see n. 5 below. On the history and growth of the Vatican libraries see J. Bignami Odier, *La Bibliothèque Vaticane de Sixte IV A Pio XI* (Città del Vaticano, 1973), chaps. 6 and 7 especially. Holstenius, Odier relates, was a "familier de la maison Barberini" (p. 111), brought to Rome in 1627 by Francesco Barberini, himself a great collector. Holstenius lived in the Barberini palazzo, and was chief librarian there from 1636. The Vatican Library received many notable acquisitions in the earlier part of the 17C; and by 1636 it had become necessary to separate the main library from the archives. Although Holstenius did not become chief custodian until 1653, he was early associated with it. He was an eminent scholar and able diplomat. One of his achievements at the Vatican was the creation of the famous frescoed Map Gallery (the long gallery leading to the Stanze)—itself a work of art. It may well have been Holstenius who procured Milton's invitation to the Palazzo Barberini.

4 Milton's letter is translated by P. Tillyard, *Milton: Private Correspondence* (Cambridge, 1932), see pp. 19-21; 125-26. Also see J. M. French, *The Life Records of J. Milton*, 5 vols. (New Brunswick, N.J., 1949-58), I, p. 391. The

original holograph was discovered and published by J. McG. Bottkol, "The Holograph of Milton's letter to Holstenius", *P.M.L.A.*, LXVIII (1953), pp. 617-27. The manuscript, purchased from the Barberini Library (filed there apparently by Holstenius himself), was brought to the Vatican Library in 1902.

5 J. Shearman has demonstrated ("The Vatican Stanze: Functions and Decoration," *Proc. Brit. Acad.*, LVII, 1971, pp. 369-424) that the Segnatura had been reconstructed and repainted c. 1507-13, as part of the general programme of reconstruction of the papal apartments conducted under Julius II. That the room was intended as a personal library to house the Pope's collection of 220 books is consistent not only with the decorative scheme but with other internal architectural features. However, Julius died in 1513; his library was incorporated into the main Vatican collection; and this Stanza (No. 14 on Shearman's plan) apparently converted to other uses. In the 1540's, in Vasari's time, it was evidently in use briefly as the chamber for one of the papal tribunals (the 'Signatura gratiae'): hence its later name. Raphael was closely concerned with the decoration of both the Stanza della Segnatura (No. 14) and the adjacent Stanza dell'Eliodoro (No. 13). The vault of the Eliodoro has an unusual design, with four sections or panels, showing Jacob's vision of the golden stairs; the burning bush, with Moses and God; Abraham's sacrifice; and God appearing to Noah. A third room in the suite, the Stanza dell'Incendio (No. 15) has a ceiling by Raphael's teacher, Perugino, of a general design not dissimilar to Raphael's vault in the Segnatura: i.e., four associated *tondi* figures illustrating "the integrity, plenitude and spiritual grace of divine justice, and its transmission... through its head" (Shearman, p. 379).

6 See the autobiographical passages in Milton's *The Reason of Church-government urg'd against Prelaty*, ed. H. Ayres, in *The Works of John Milton* (Columbia ed., New York, 1931-38), 18 vols., Vol. III, pt. 1 (1931), p. 235; and *Second Defence of the People of England*, transl. G. Burnett, Vol. VIII (1933), pp. 121-29. All subsequent references to Milton's prose, and quotations, are taken from the Columbia edition. Milton records in these tracts that Manso himself conducted him around Naples and that in Rome Milton viewed the antiquities. See also W. R. Parker, "Notes on Italy, 1638-1639", Vol. II, pp. 818-22; "Italy, 1638-1639", Vol. I, pp. 176-77.

7 Access to the Papal apartments may have been more difficult in the sixteenth century: accounting perhaps for Vasari's problems—on which see among others E. H. Gombrich, "Raphael's *Stanza della Segnatura* and the Nature of its Symbolism", *Symbolic Images: Studies in the Art of the Renaissance* (London, 1972), p. 85 and n. 4. Not so, apparently, by the mid-seventeenth century: see R. Frye, *Milton's Imagery and the Visual Arts: Iconographic Tradition in the Epic Poems* (Princeton, 1978), pp. 27ff.

8 Frye, pp. 27-28, notes specifically that the wall paintings in the Vatican complex were listed in guidebooks of the 1630's as "available for viewing"—even to visitors without Milton's influential friends—and that contemporary travel accounts indicate that such opportunities were freely taken.

34 sheets of engravings of Raphael's ceilings were in print by 1607 and are known to have been in England in 1650-51.

[9] Frye, p. 25. For Milton's own evidence on this, see n. 6 above.

[10] Parker, Vol. II, p. 820, summarizes. It is worth noting that Milton nowhere alludes to music in his account of Italy: yet we know from E. Phillips, *The Life of Mr. John Milton* (1694), (see *The Early Lives of Milton*, ed. H. Darbishire, London, 1932, p. 59), that Milton had sent back from Venice for the highly musical Milton household "a Chest or two of choice Musick-books of the best Masters".

[11] Frye in his second chapter reviews some of the critical literature from the eighteenth century to the present. Of interest on Milton's relationship to Italian painting are: A. Stein, "Milton and Metaphysical Art: an Exploration", *E.L.H.*, 16 (1949); H. Gardner, *A Reading of Paradise Lost* (Oxford, 1965); J. H. Hanford (see n. 12 below); C. A. Patrides, "John Milton: The Poet who Gave us Paradise", The Observer (Colour Supplement), 13 August 1969, pp. 3-9; and Amy Lee Turner, *The Visual Arts in Milton's Poetry*, Rice Univ. Ph.D. diss., 1955.

For a list of critical works on Milton's relationship to the visual arts, iconography and painting, see: *Milton*, annot. bibl. compiled by J. H. Hanford and Wm. A. McQueen, 2nd ed. (Chapel Hill, N.C., 1979). This substantial list reveals that interest has centred largely on: the illustrators of Milton; Blake and Milton; Poussin (comparisons of Milton's landscapes to); portraiture of Milton; Milton and English art; general studies of 'the baroque'; the broad traditions of iconography behind particular scenes relating to the Fall, the Tree, the Expulsion, etc.—see e.g., J. B. Trapp, "Iconography", in *John Milton: Introductions*, ed. J. Broadbent (Cambridge, 1973), pp. 162-85, and "The Iconography of the Fall of Man" in *Approaches to Paradise Lost: The York Tercentenary Lectures*, ed. C. A. Patrides (London, 1968), pp. 223-65. Frye's book extends this direction of inquiry. It can be seen that there have been almost no attempts to correlate specific passages in *PL* with particular paintings. Yet contrast Hanford's intuition: see n. 12 below.

[12] J. H. Hanford, *John Milton, Englishman* (New York, 1949; London, 1950), p. 97 (cited by Parker, II, pp. 820-21):

> He [Milton] nowhere alludes to the work of the great painters which must have confronted him everywhere. But *Paradise Lost* is best illustrated by comparison with these analogous expressions, and its fusion of Christian and pagan imagery, its visualizations of Biblical legend and of classical mythology, its rich perspectives and its profusion of detail, are probably more indebted than Milton himself realized to what his eyes took in on the ceilings [*sic*] of the Sistine Chapel or the walls of the Doge's palace.

See also J. H. Hanford, *Annuale Mediaevale* (1964), p. 63. Frye notes (p. 17, n. 46) that "in private conversations Professor Hanford expressed even more hope than in his published works" about finding evidence on this matter.

[13] J. B. Trapp: see n. 11 above.

[14] Frye, p. 4.

15 See Frye, p. 15 and n. 37.

16 Frye, pp. 4-5.

17 Frye, pp. 171-73 and *passim.*

18 Frye, pp. 209-11.

19 The details noted by Frye include: the apple with the *bough*—perhaps based on Raphael (p. 289); the trees of gold in 'The Disputà', suggestive of Milton's Eden (p. 253); the palm tree, mentioned by Milton as growing in Eden, seen in the 'Creation of the Animals' (p. 243); and the globe of angels surrounding Christ in the 'Disputà' (here a conventional detail, as in many paintings)—recalling *PL* III. 60-62, V. 594-96, 631 and *Paradise Regained* I. 171 and IV. 581-83 (p. 184). The theme of 'descents' of angels (as in Raphael's 'St. Michael', see p. 172) offers a striking visual analogy to many situations in *PL*, such as Raphael's flight in Book V.

20 Frye, pp. 161-62 and nn. 46-47. The idea probably comes originally from Lucretius, Bk V.

21 Gombrich, "Aims and Limits of Iconology", *Symbolic Images*, p. 6.

22 Cf. Milton (cited Frye, p. 34): "there are in a picture two things—the *subject or archetype* and the art of painting", *Art of Logic*, XI (1935), p. 11; italics mine.

23 On the cases against and for programmes dictated by humanist 'advisers', see, respectively, C. Hope, "Artists, Patrons, and Advisers in the Italian Renaissance", in *Patronage in the Renaissance*, ed. G. F. Lytle and S. Orgel (Princeton, 1981), pp. 293-343; and C. Robertson, "Annibal Caro as Iconographer: Sources and Method", *J. W. C. I.*, XLV (1982), pp. 160-81. The argument seems to turn not so much on the existence or use of such programmes from before 1500 to 1550 or later (we have only to glance at Alberti's stress as early as 1450 on the need for literary 'inventions' in paintings; see App. I), as on the degree to which artists were or were not constrained by them, or allowed to contribute their own ideas. There seems to be no reason why eminent artists especially should not sometimes have adapted programmes, contributed their own ideas, or allowed the 'meanings' fairly freely to evolve. Indeed, there is every reason to think that sometimes it might have been impossible for them to do otherwise. (See n. 7, chap. 4, on the evolution of Raphael's 'Disputà'.) It would seem probable that at as early a date as 1507-08, and in the complex and changing physical circumstances surrounding Raphael's painting of the Stanza della Segnatura, he could scarcely have worked according to a wholly and externally predetermined programme. I do not think that this probability interferes with the hypothesis of a complex 'invention' in the Stanza, to which others may have contributed themes or details, but which was adapted and expanded by Raphael and evolved under his hand.

24 Gombrich, "Aims and Limits of Iconology", *Symbolic Images*, pp. 6-7.

25 See Gombrich's analysis of the mediaeval origins but much more developed and complex programme evolved in the allegorical design of the Stanza della Segnatura, *Symbolic Images*, pp. 85-101. J. Shearman, *Proc. Brit. Acad.*, pp.

410-11, n. 86, traces the German scholarship on the history and iconographical antecedents of the room.

26 Gombrich, "Appendix: Annibale Caro's *Programme* for Taddeo Zuccaro . . .", in *Symbolic Images*, pp. 23-25.

27 On *ut pictura poesis*, see App. I.

28 This does not coincide with the interpretation of the spatial relations by J. Shearman on p. 141 of 'The Chigi Chapel in S. Maria del Popolo', *J. W.C.I.*, XXIV (1961), pp. 129-60. Yet this does seem to an observer to be the visual impression communicated by the painting.

29 Shearman, *ibid.*, p. 142.

30 Shearman, *ibid.*, pp. 140-42, offers a Neoplatonic-Christian interpretation, connected with the life of the soul after death (and thus with the funerary nature of the chapel).

31 Conversation, Pat Rubin.

32 Summarizing 'The Disputà', G. P. Bellori, *Descrizzione Delle Imagini dipinte da Rafaelle d'Urbino* (Rome, 1695: republ. [facs.] Farnborough, Hants., 1968), p. 13.

33 It is agreed that Pope Julius II prescribed the subject. This might have been done in a general way, and perhaps accounts for the strong emphasis on Justice in the room (see chap. 2, n. 13)—although the Stanza's rôle as a tribunal chamber apparently was not fixed at the time Raphael painted. J. Pope-Hennessy (*Raphael: The Wrightsman Lectures*, Vol. 4, London: Phaidon, n.d., p. 139) on rather slight grounds proposes as a source the works of Bonaventura (via 'a Franciscan monk'). L. Dussler, *Raphael: A Critical Catalogue of his Pictures, Wall-Paintings and Tapestries* (London and New York, 1971), p. 70, is sceptical.

34 See Dussler, p. 70; and J. Pope-Hennessy, p. 148: "It is likely therefore that the four Allegories represent not the concepts in the painter's or the patron's mind at the time the frescoes were commissioned, but a classical summation of the message of the room when three of the four frescoes were complete. It is as though the mind or minds which had guided Raphael through the scholastic maze of the programme of the walls reformulated the whole intellectual basis of the scheme". Shearman (see n. 5 above) gives a full history of the evolution of the Stanza's architecture and decoration.

35 Gombrich, "Raphael's *Stanza della Segnatura*", *Symbolic Images*, p. 88, uses this term and also 'amplification'.

36 An echo of G. B. Adriani, friend of Vasari, in a letter to Cosimo I (1550's), which I give in paraphrase. (Eng. transl. in C. Hope, pp. 334-35; Italian, pp. 335-36, n. 79.) Adriani stresses not only the close ideational relationship between painting and poetry, but the importance of a corresponding erudition in the beholder, saying that a picture of a new subject is more pleasing when one already has some prior idea about it: that is, when one can easily make out the rest from what one already brings to a painting, so that each may feel that he has discovered th meaning for himself.

37 Bellori uses the term 'imagini'; as does the title of that favourite Renaissance handbook, V. Cartari's *Le Imagini de i Dei de gli Antichi*... (Venice, 1571), in facs. series 'The Renaissance and the Gods', ed. S. Orgel (New York and London, 1976), Vol. 12.

NOTES TO CHAPTER II

1 Gombrich, "Aims and Limits of Iconology", *Symbolic Images*, p. 6.

2 The vocabulary is similar to that used by Boccaccio, Tasso, Sidney, Milton and many other writers of the fourteenth to seventeenth centuries in their critical discussions of poetry. Their vocabulary and views are shared exactly by the painters (see App. I). The argument over the importance of allegory ('meanings') in painting (or in poetry) is too far-reaching to enter into here: it partly rests on too narrow an understanding of the concept of 'allegory' in the Renaissance or before. But one may stress again the importance of the fact that the ancient and even the Italian classics were very commonly read (and translated) in contemporary editions with extensive critical commentaries which largely took the form of allegorical interpretation. (Ovid, Ariosto and Tasso came into English translation c. 1600 or before in such editions.) Allegory is thus embedded in the very way the ancient or modern texts communicated to poets, painters and readers (and this even without the further sources of allegorical dictionaries and handbooks). (Cf. Robertson, p. 166, discussing Caro's sources, and Hope, p. 313, discussing Bernini, on the use by both painters of Italian commentaries on Ovid.) From the literary end of the spectrum, Robertson's contention (pp. 172, 175) that iconographical 'invenzione' in Renaissance painting could be almost synonymous with poetic invention understood in the conceptual sense (often implying a heavily allegorized sense) finds ample support.

3 Vasari, *Vite*, IV, 'Vita da Raffaello...': on the Stanza, pp. 166-74. (In Eng. transl., Everyman, London and New York: n.d., 2, pp. 226-30.)

4 Much is explained as to the dissatisfaction one may feel over Vasari's essentially uninterpretative account of the Stanza by the simple fact that, as P. Rubin puts it, he was not an iconographer. In this he was himself reacting perhaps against earlier more philosophical accounts and interpretations. This notwithstanding his admiration of Raphael's 'inspiration', and of A. Caro's 'ingenious invention' in the Camera dell'Aurora (as cited from the *Vite*, by Robertson, p. 160).

5 On the last point, see Gombrich, "Raphael's *Stanza della Segnatura*", *Symbolic Images*, p. 89. My impression is that critics may not always have apprehended this aspect of the Stanza's complexity: if Raphael consciously dovetailed several different schemes or different kinds of programme into the room, as it evolved, then certain seeming contradictions as to 'meaning' disappear.

6 Against this empty space, occupied only by *divini amori* (as in the Chigi Chapel) and which can only represent heaven, floats the coat of arms of Pope Nicholas VI—a detail which will not please critics of a strongly protestant

sensibility, but which I think Milton, who was fairly strong-minded, might have managed to ignore. It is not irrelevant to add that the positioning of the *putti* holding the coat of arms clearly shows it to be floating *in front of* and not *in* the heavenly space. The roundel is not usually attributed to Raphael: but he retained and made use of it as the focus of his design on the vault.

7 Gombrich, "Raphael's *Stanza della Segnatura*", *Symbolic Images*, p. 92.

8 *Ibid.*, p. 88. The inscriptions read: Poetry, *numine afflatur*, 'the divine inspiration'; Theology, *divinar[um] rer[um] notitia*, 'knowledge of things divine'; Justice, *ius suum unicuique tribuit*, 'to each his due'; and Philosophy, *causarum cognitio*, 'knowledge of causes'. Dussler (p. 70) locates those of Theology and Justice in Justinian; those of Philosophy and Poetry in Virgil. N. Rash-Fabbri, "A Note on the Stanza della Segnatura", *Gazette des Beaux-Arts*, XCIV (1979), pp. 97-104, finds that the *titulus* of Philosophy also could relate to Justinian; while the phrase itself comes from Cicero.

9 Bellori, pp. 26-27.

10 Bellori, pp. 4-5. "E la Virtù", Bellori somewhat vaguely adds (Gombrich follows, p. 88; see n. 8 above). This uncertainty may arise simply because (as Gombrich himself notes passingly) Raphael is in fact conflating more than one 'scheme' in the Stanza: in this context, Justice as one of the cardinal *virtues* on the window wall, with Justice as also a form of Wisdom or Knowledge on the ceiling (in human study, Jurisprudence—a distinction that Bellori is careful to sustain). Overall the Stanza continues to exhibit Raphael's firm exposition of the unity of all human knowledges as reflections of the divine.

11 Vasari, *Vite*, IV, pp. 168-70 (Everyman, 2, pp. 227-28). Only with 'Astrology' does Vasari seem uncertain how to correlate the rectangle with any specific *tondo* figure: she often seems to be perceived as difficult.

12 Vasari's well-known error in conflating 'The Disputà' with 'The School of Athens' does not invalidate the whole of his opening remarks (*Vite*, IV, p. 166; rep. p. 168; Everyman, 2, p. 227)—although his confusion over the wall frescoes is clearly evident in the ensuing description. 'Reconciliation' takes place, yes; but it is not the theologians but (implicitly) *God* who 'reconciles', or to use Gombrich's translation (p. 85), "harmonizes". Does Vasari's bracketing of Philosophy, Theology and Astrology (leaving out Justice) suggest some special importance attaching not only to the 'harmonizing' on the whole vault, but also in that particular corner connecting Philosophy, Astrology and in fact Poetry? The latter is omitted perhaps because the inclusion of Poetry is more difficult to account for. She often seems to be an 'also ran'; note the care Bellori takes over his words: "la Teologia, la Filosofia, la Giurisprudenza, ò sia la Giustitia, & *insieme la Poesia*, ciascuna accommodata al fine medesimo", p. 4 (italics mine). Again, to the three "imagini" on the ceiling, Theology, Jurisprudence and Philosophy, all "mediatrici" of Wisdom, "*fù aggiunta* la quarta... della Poesia" (p. 27). But Bellori later finds a better reason why Poetry can properly be included in the great conception: because in antiquity all the other sciences derived, as from a fount, from the

Poets (p. 27). (Many other reasons could be given to account for her presence in a library dedicated to knowledge.) In any case, cf. the 15C 'Liberal Arts' series of engravings, cited in App. III, where 'Poesia' *is* included.

13 E. Wind, "Platonic Justice, Designed by Raphael", *J. W.C.I.*, I (1937-38), pp. 69-70, sees a 'concordance' of knowledge and of virtues in the scheme of the room with Justice as the master virtue, or in platonic terms the "harmony of the virtues" (from *Rep.* IV, 432 ff. and *Nich. Eth.* V. 3). The idea of more than one kind of 'concordance' in the room seems right: but not that of Justice as the dominant concept of the entire room (despite its special importance on the ceiling and especially elevated place on the 'Justice' wall—see Dussler, p. 70; N. Rash-Fabbri, pp. 97-98; and n. 8 above). The special place of Justice may express a compliment to the Papal rôle: but to make it the "master virtue" of all necessarily disbalances the focus of the ceiling on the divine as source of all forms of *knowledge*. What seems to be emerging, as we delve into the Stanza's meaning, is a continuing amalgamation of a number of subordinate programmes (in this case, Justice as the 'harmony of the *virtues*' on the portion of the wall above the window; and on the vault, Justice as a scheme reconciling divine and human *laws*, the Justinian context being important here) into the larger scheme of the room as a whole, which itself offers four parallel enlargements of the 'Liberal Arts' cycle concept, all of them 'reconciled' into the larger or divine unity represented by the ceiling's 'summation'.

14 My view synthesizes from a number of critics, including those already quoted, and perhaps adds some further inflections. For a comprehensive bibliography, see L. Dussler. A more recent summation of critical thinking is J. Pope-Hennessy's. The latter's stance is indicative of continuing uncertainty about the nature of the Stanza's message. Although Gombrich asks if the Stanza has not been *over*-interpreted, he means, I think, in ways which fragment it.

15 Vasari, *Vite*, IV, pp. 166-70 (Everyman, 2, pp. 227-28).

16 See n. 8 above.

17 It is important to recognize that poetry too was seen as a form of wisdom (and religion)—especially divine (Christian) poetry—and that poetic inspiration was seen as closely connected with prophetic inspiration. The Bible contains inspired prophecy, and inspired poetry in the Psalms and elsewhere. Homer (to the ancients a bible) is placed by Raphael prominently on the Parnassus, beneath Poetry in her globe. Toscanella (cited Gombrich, "Raphael's *Stanza della Segnatura*", *Symbolic Images*, pp. 89-90) says that poets first affirmed God and his rule and cites Orpheus as an antique theologian along with Homer (see chap 3, n. 8). Also, poets have praised virtue through their fictions: an idea as old as Dante and Boccaccio. In the Invocation to *PL*, Bk. III, Milton includes mention of *Orpheus*, Thamyris and Maeonides (Homer) with "*Tiresias* and *Phineus* Prophets old" (lines 17; 35-36). In Bk. VII. 37-38 he (in lines identifying himself with that figure) alludes to Orpheus. In Bk. I. 8 he cites Moses. Thus Milton too has bracketed, in the unified contexts of the Invocations, poetry and prophecy: brought together Moses, Orpheus, Homer,

other poets and himself, as examples of prophets/law-givers/poets/priests. Other prophetic motifs enter elsewhere. Cf. also Milton's utterance in *Of Reformation Touching Church-Discipline in England*, ed. H. Ayres, Vol. III, pt. 1 (1931), p. 78, on the priest-like rôle of the poet.

18 See chap. 4, and especially nn. 4 and 7.

19 In the adjacent Stanza dell'Incendio (Shearman's room 15), Justice's sword points down.

20 Bellori, p. 7.

21 Gombrich, "Raphael's *Stanza della Segnatura*", *Symbolic Images*, p. 94, cites J. D. Passavant as being the first to interpret the rectangles as linking the various Faculties. Dussler (p. 71) also finds on the whole secular connections. My impression is that many or most critics have not recognized a double linkage as operative across the entire vault, and as functioning at a number of quite different levels.

22 Dussler on the other hand (p. 71) sees the Apollo-Marsyas scene as referring to "the flouting of divine authority". In the 15C engraving in the Tarocchi series (see chap. 6, n. 20), Apollo is shown enthroned: which supports Dussler's view. Yet the regal Apollo is but one constituent theme in Raphael's much more complex painting.

23 E. Wind, "The Flaying of Marsyas" in *Pagan Mysteries in the Renaissance* (first publ. London, 1958; 2nd enlarged ed., London, 1968), p. 172, n. 6, notes that Raphael's figure of Marsyas corresponds almost literally with the antique statue of Marsyas on the Capitoline; this need not have precluded a Christianized development of the theme.

24 From the poem by Du Bartas (l. 58) at the end of my final chapter.

25 *Wind.*, pp. 171-76. Wind calls the Raphael rectangle "an example of Poetic Theology representing a mystery of the pagans" (p. 175). On poetic theology, see chap. 3, n. 8. A more secular strain of early Renaissance humanist interpretation at least as early as the 15C seeks a geographical allusion in the Marsyas story (the satyrs wept to form the river of that name). See entry, 'Marsyas', in *Metamorphoses* (Lyons, 1516), Bk. VI, fo. LXXXVI, in series *The Renaissance and the Gods*, Vol. 3 (1976). Similarly Cartari. Raphael is clearly not employing any so secular interpretation: the answer may well lie in earlier moralized commentaries.

26 J. Baudouin says of 'Astrologie', in his transl. of C. Ripa, *Iconologie* (Paris, 1644), p. 24, that "cette Science a cela de propre, *d'eslever l'esprit* aux connoissances les plus louables & les plus hautes" (italics mine). In this instance, the 'Astrologie' figure he glosses is *winged.*

27 Traditionally the lesser 'Urania' is the figure seated on the ground to the right of Apollo; he also is seated; both are gazing upward. Dussler, p. 74, identifies a different figure as Urania (the one standing with back to us). It makes no difference to the present point: all the Parnassus figures seem indolent.

28 Bellori evidently connects the rectangles to the ladies on their *right* hand: excepting 'Urania', who remains for him unattached. Vasari seems to connect certain rectangles to the *left*.

29 Small wonder that Bellori (p. 13)—although thinking particularly of 'The Disputà'—spoke of Raphael's inspired invention and said that Raphael himself must have participated in the divine mind: "In sì grandi, e divini misteri Rafaelle istesso non senza divino afflato, si dimostrò partecipe di celeste mente, spiegandoci col pennello le sue sopraumane idee".

30 Pat Rubin draws my attention to the fact that blank tablets are a known (if unexplained) feature in Renaissance paintings: as e.g., those held by the *putti* flanking the Virgin in Raphael's 'Madonna di Foligno' (originally the high altarpiece at S. Maria in Aracoeli in Rome). Blank books seem analogous.

31 *Vite*, JV, p. 170; Everyman, 2, p. 228. Vasari's wording could signify either that divine prescience which made the universe, or merely astronomy. The Everyman transl. is misleading in calling the 'Urania' figure a 'science'; Vasari does not use the word 'science'.

32 More clearly by Bellori's description of the figure than by his philosophical exposition: see n. 34 below, and text. Dussler calls the figure 'the universe' (p. 70), and ascribes the name 'Urania'. For E. Winner's interpretation, see n. 35 below.

33 The problem over the name and role of 'Astrology' (and Raphael's figure) runs a long way back. We may understand Vasari's earlier use of the name 'Astrology' a little more readily, inasmuch as in the Renaissance that concept or science possessed a semi-divine status which the term no longer conveys to us today. There are at least two differing emblem representations of 'Astrology' in Ripa: the one stressing her authority (sceptre, eagle); the other showing her as winged. Both figures have a starry crown and starry globe. Their attributes also overlap with cognate figures (Poesy, Urania, Theology). See Appendix III.

34 Bellori, p. 7; the description illustrates his habitual sensitivity.

35 The long mediaeval and neoplatonic tradition linking Contemplation and the *vita passiva*, as in Dante, or as exemplified by the Lady Philosophy in Boethius, has been suggested by E. Winner (Paper: Warburg Institute, London, 26 November 1983) as leading to a further identification of Raphael's 'Astrology' with the 'Mens Divina' and hence in Christian terms with 'Providenzia'. This is an important perception.

NOTES TO CHAPTER III

1 Quotations from *Paradise Lost* (henceforth *PL*) follow the text of H. Darbishire, *The Poetical Works of John Milton*, 2 Vols. (Oxford, 1952-55), Vol. I, *Paradise Lost* (Oxford, 1952). Italics, except with proper or place names, are my own.

2 See *Gerusalemme liberata*, I. vii: as in Fairfax's translation, *Godfrey of Bulloigne*, 1600 (= *Jerusalem Delivered*), ed. K. Lea and T. Gang (Oxford, 1981).

[3] Earlier, evidently, this largish circle used to be taken for the earth: but it is not, as closer inspection reveals. Milton too knows that the Earth is much smaller and "not unconform to other shining Globes" (*PL*, V. 259). It is very interesting that Milton's universe also has the precision and concreteness of a working model: like an orrery, it both 'moves' and 'works'. A. Fowler in his ed. of *PL* (*The Poems of John Milton*, ed. J. Carey and A. Fowler, London, 1968; repr. as *Paradise Lost*, 1971) has noted many instances of astronomical functionality in Milton's universe. See also M. Sarkar, "'The Visible Diurnal Sphere': Astronomical Images of Space and Time in *Paradise Lost*", *MQ*, 18 (1984), pp. 1-5.

[4] R. Jones and N. Penny, *Raphael* (Yale, 1983), p. 108, say that the emphasis conveyed is on 'hopes for the afterlife', Elijah being associated with the Ascension. *Did* Milton see the Chigi chapel at S. Maria del Popolo? If he did not, he missed what was in the early 16C said to "surpass all others in Rome", and a century later, still to have the "grandest reputation" and to be "the most visited in Rome by connoisseurs". (See Penny, p. 111, citing a guide-book of 1517 and a 17C member of the Chigi family.) This was even before Bernini "put the finishing touches to it" (two statues), after 1627. The chapel's final improvements (according to Shearman, *J.W.C.I.*, 1961, pp. 130-31 and n. 15) were planned by 1627 and completed by c. 1653. This means that Milton's visit (1638-39) came at a time when this famous church and chapel were recently and prominently again in the public attention.

[5] See A. Fowler's ed., nn. to *PL*, III. 555-61.

[6] Jacob's Ladder was a common enough iconographic motif. There is also in the Loggia a ceiling panel (school of Raphael) showing, in much smaller scale, a sleeping Jacob, with the stairs seen centre picture. It is a much less interesting composition, and there is no 'open sky'. See Frye, Plate 136, for a mediaeval illustration of the Stairs.

[7] 'Raptus' is also an older medical term for 'fit' (epilepsy).

[8] It is perhaps significant that an early description (1542) of Mantegna's 'Parnassus' takes or mistakes the Apollo figure playing for "*Orpheus* playing" to the nymphs (see Gombrich, "An Interpretation of Mantegna's 'Parnassus'", *Symbolic Images*, p. 83, and p. 220, n. 8): perhaps because the two figures were allegorically interchangeable. Gombrich in the same volume ("Raphael's *Stanza della Segnatura*", p. 89) notes that Toscanella praises "Orpheus, whom the ancients also considered a theologian". A more substantial discussion of "Orpheus the Theologian and Renaissance Platonists" is that by D. P. Walker, *J.W.C.I.*, XVI (1953), pp. 100-20. Cf. also E. Wind, "Poetic Theology", in *Pagan Mysteries*, pp. 18, 21, 24 esp. J. M. Evans discusses Milton's use of the Orpheus legend in chap. 5 of *The Road from Horton: Looking Backwards in "Lycidas"*, *ELS* Monograph series, no. 28 (University of Victoria, B.C., 1983).

[9] For a discussion of the literature on Urania and the Invocations, see App. II.

[10] As cited by Hunter, p. 39, from *The Christian Doctrine (De Doctrina Christiana)*, I. 3, transl. C. Sumner; ed. J. H. Hanford and W. H. Dunn, XIV (1933), p. 65; italics mine.

11 See *The Christian Doctrine*, I. 7, as quoted in n. 12 below.

12 Two allusions, one from Hughes (p. 14), the other from Hunter (*S.E.L.*, p. 39), are illuminating. Speaking of Milton's Wisdom, sister of Urania, and Spenser's 'Sapience' (a near relation), Hughes notes the connection "Most obviously [with] the Wisdom which Solomon quoted as saying that before the creation she was with God 'as one brought up with him... daily his delight, playing always before him'" (*Proverbs*, 8.30). Through this we can understand how Milton sees the two figures of Urania (divine Muse) and Wisdom (divine) as united in the presence of God (Raphael's perception is similar). Now Milton remarks of the eighth chapter of *Proverbs* that it is not, in his opinion, the Son of God who speaks there, but "a poetical personification of wisdom" (*The Christian Doctrine*, I. 7, XV, 1933, p. 13). 'Personifications', whether poetical or in painting, are part of the iconographical vocabulary of both artists (they are not thereby, of course, merely 'fictions').

The other interesting distinction is quoted by Hunter (*S.E.L.*, pp. 39-40, via C. Patrides) from J. Prideaux "concerning the equivalence of Christ and Wisdom..." (*Wisdomes Justification: a Sermon preached at the court*, Oxford, 1636, p. 8). I give the passage in slightly fuller context:

> Words of an *ambiguous meaning*, must bee first *distinguished*, before they can be *defined*,... Of this *sort*, is this *word*, *wisdome*,... [it] may bee understood, either to be, *Divine*, or *Humane*. *Divine* sometimes designes *Christ* himselfe, the *second Person* in the *Trinity*.... *Otherwhere*, & more *often*, it notes the infinite *skill* of the most *high*, in *creating*, & *perfecting* all *things*, and by his *Providence*, ordering them, to their appointed *ends*, and *uses*.

Here we have conjoined the cognate notions of Providence as an ordering aspect of God's wisdom; Wisdom, as in designing the universe and perfecting it (not wholly separable from the divine Contemplation, perhaps); and Wisdom as the second Person—all aspects of 'divine... Wisdom'. Again we may think of the several aspects of Raphael's 'Urania' (and probably Milton's) and their close ties with Philosophy or Wisdom. Clearly it was a commonplace for earlier periods to think in such ways.

NOTES TO CHAPTER IV

1 On the Urania-figure, see Dussler, and chap. 2, n. 27.

2 For a summary of identifications see Dussler, pp. 74-75.

3 What do the conspicuously different sizes and bindings of some of the books signify? One might have thought possibly some of the different main versions of the Bible. However, Jerome is not included in Dussler's list of identifications, pp. 71-72. The four Gospels in the central panel of the 'Disputà' are shown as of equal size and shape.

4 *Vite*, IV, p. 171 (Everyman, 2, p. 229).

5 Dussler, p. 72.

6 The Council of Trent, between 1540-60, promulgated as definite doctrines the concepts of the Sacraments and of transubstantiation. Such specific emphases did not exist in pre-Reformation theology.

7 Gombrich, "Raphael's *Stanza della Segnatura*", *Symbolic Images*, p. 91. It is known from the preliminary drawings and sketches and their alterations that the altar and Host were a later addition, included in the course of Raphael's working out of his compositional dilemmas over the design. Because the fresco of the 'Disputà' is painted on the higher part of the wall, the impression is given that the viewer walks towards the altar. But this part of the painting although at eye-level is the much less dramatic component. It is the central triptych of gold in the upper panel, with the stylized Christ and Dove, which Raphael developed after discarding his first sketches of a naturalistic Christ drawn to the same scale as the adjacent Apostles and Patriarchs to right and left, that arrests the eye and forms the visual centre of the painting. This point is reinforced by the first sketches for the lower part of the painting (see P. Joannides, *Raphael*, Oxford, 1983, p. 182), which show that where the altar now is shown, flanked by gazing and marvelling doctors or dignitaries, Raphael had drawn at first four seated (? Apostles) looking at open books, or else gazing upward from their books, as if seeking illumination—a treatment which is in keeping with the figures flanking Christ in the upper part. On the evolution of "The Disputà', see also J. White, "Raphael and Bruegel: Two Aspects of the Relationship between Form and Content", *The Burlington Magazine*, CIII (1961), 230-35; also Penny, pp. 59-61.

8 Gombrich, as in n. 7 above. However, the idea of the vertical triptych was already to hand in the design of the Perugino vault in the adjacent Stanza dell' Incendio. One of the four *tondi* there shows a Father above a Son (both surrounded by gold) above a white Dove, in the same descending arrangement that Raphael also employs.

9 Preface to *The Christian Doctrine*, XIV, p. 11.

10 D. C. Allen's description and analysis in "Milton and the Descent to Light", *J.E.G.P.*, LX (1961), pp. 614-30, has a different orientation and does not trace this sequence.

11 See chap. 3, n. 8, and text.

NOTES TO CHAPTER V

1 See *The Christian Doctrine*, I. 6: quotations from XIV, pp. 357-403.

2 See *Milton's Commonplace Book*, entry 'De Poetica', Vol. XVIII (1938), ed. J. H. Hanford, p. 139:

> Basil tells us that poetry was given by God to rouse in human souls the love of virtue. 'For when the Holy Spirit saw that mankind could be led with difficulty to virtue... what did it do? It mixed with the dogmas the pleasure of poetry...'.

3 There is undoubtedly some misunderstanding on this point (see articles cited in App. II) as to whether or not the Holy Spirit may properly be 'invoked' (therefore by extrapolation properly be addressed in Milton's 'Invocations'). Milton says that the Spirit may not be 'invoked' as *personality* (third Person) but that the 'gifts' of the spirit or Spirit may nonetheless be 'sought'

or 'solicited' (if directly prayed for, then Milton probably intends to the Son or—I think—the Father). It is not Milton who has given the proems the accolade of 'Invocations' (in the religious sense): such a use or word appears nowhere in *PL*. The four proems all suggest various or varying literary forms: rhetorical *invocatio*; salutation or prayer; 'solicitation' (of hoped-for 'gifts'); meditation; personal musings; expression of personal hopes (and fears); prologuizing; and technical discussions of poetry.

NOTES TO CHAPTER VI

1 Fairfax transl., I. ii. Fairfax adds the detail of the spring to Tasso's 'Helicon' —possibly after 'Sion's spring' in Du Bartas (see n. 13 below).

2 Some older Italian editors have named her as the Virgin; but there is absolutely nothing to support such an interpretation.

3 For Du Bartas see the edition of U. T. Holmes, Jr., J. C. Lyons and R. W. Linker, *The Works of Guillaume de Salluste Sieur Du Bartas: a critical edition*..., 3 vols. (Chapel Hill, N.C., 1935-40), Vol. II, containing *La Muse Chrestiene* (the original edition of poems in which appeared "L'Uranie") and *La Creation du Monde ou Premiere Sepmaine*. The earlier "L'Uranie" takes the form of a lament by the Muse. The two *Sepmaines* (only) are included in J. Sylvester's translation, ed. S. Snyder: *The Divine Weeks and Works of Guillaume de Saluste Sieur Du Bartas* (Oxford, 1979), 2 vols. Sylvester did however translate the earlier Du Bartas poem also. Quotations are taken from these two editions.

4 See *Il Mondo Creato*: crit. ed. of G. Petrocchi (Florence, 1951), *Primo Giorno*, lines 1-27; q. fr. line 20. The entire passage, lines 1-27 and ff., finds many echoes also in the other Invocations and elsewhere in *PL*.

5 Hughes: see App. II. On Du Bartas and Milton: see L. B. Campbell, App. II, and G. C. Taylor, *Milton's Use of Du Bartas* (Cambridge, Mass., 1934), chap. 1.

6 Sylvester transl., Vol. I, respectively: 'The First Day', line 7; 'The Fifth Day', line 13; 'The Sixth Day', line 17; 'The First Day', line 13 (Sylvester's addition); 'The Seventh Day', line 49; 'The Third Day', line 13; 'The Fifth Day', line 17.

7 Vol I, 'The Third Day', lines 1, 9. Here like and unlike Milton's "Standing on Earth...", *PL*, VII. 23.

8 Vol. I, 'The Third Day', line 2. In 'The Fifth Day', line 21, it is the "Lord" who is asked to "teach me dyve"; but J. Hall (see n. 13 below) transfers this thought to the Sylvestrian Urania.

9 In the French ed., Vol. II, 'Le Quatriesme Jour', line 1, and 'Le Troisiesme Jour', line 1.

10 At the opening of 'The Fourth Day', Vol. I, Sylvester does give "Spirit" for "Esprit".

11 'The Second Day', Vol. I, line 37. Du Bartas gives in the French (more Miltonically) 'fountain' ("surjon") as opposed to the pedestrian "source" of Sylvester: an indifferent archaism for 'spring'.

12 Vol I, 'The Second Day', line 42, and 'The I Part of the I Day of the II Week', line 29. Milton's rendering, *PL.* IX. 20, is certainly an improvement.

13 Vol. I, 'The Fourth Day', lines 1-21 and 81-82. The first line must have been famous, for it was echoed by Sylvester's admirers: see Vol. II, p. 920, for J. Hall's commendatory poem. (Hall echoes Sylvester also in the detail of "*Sions* sacred Spring", from Sylvester's additions at lines 81-82). Later Sylvester echoed himself, in a small poem (cited Vol. I, p. 8): "when *Urania* after *rapted* it" (second italics mine). Some of the most bathetic phrasings (e.g., end of line 21) are Sylvester's additions.

14 The first poem cited, in an edition (d. 151.?) of *Pontani Opera*, is entitled *Urania, sive de stellis: libri quinque.* It has the passage cited in the text (from the opening peroration). An undivided *Meteororum liber*, publ. in the modern ed. of M. de Nichilo, *I poemi astrologici di Giovanni Pontano* (Bari, 1975) also invokes 'Uranie' as the presiding Muse near the beginning and end of the poem (see p. 93, line 25; p. 137, line 101). Nichilo in his critical introduction examines the development and textual difficulties of Pontanus' astrological poems.

15 Much is conveyed by Pontanus' parenthesis invoking "*Alma* Venus" (the generative Venus of Nature and not the goddess of sexual love). "We have sung enough of the gentle fires of your son" (line 18: "teneros nati sat lusimus ignes"), from *Pontani Opera, Urania, sive de stellis*, line 18. This same thought forms the substance of the 'lament' of the Bartasian Muse in the earlier "L'Uranie" and is reiterated in the *Sepmaine.*

16 *Pontani Opera*, p. 2, lines 5-6. Italics here and in the ff. two quotations are mine. The goddess who "*takes her name from the heavens*" (in Pontanus and Du Bartas, italics mine) does so because etymologically her name derives from the Greek *houranois* (translit.), which means both 'sky', and also the celestial Heaven (as in the first line of the Greek New Testament Lord's Prayer.

17 From *La Muse Chrestienne* in *The Works of Du Bartas*, II, p. 184, "L'Uranie", lines 249-50.

18 This important echo of Pontanus has evidently not been noted by scholars: although sometimes Horace is cited (*Odes*, 3.4: "Descende caelo . . . Calliope") in connection with *PL*, VII. 1. Gombrich cites Pontanus (the passage alluded to above: see n. 16 above, and text) and I think *does* suspect a possible affinity between Mantegna's 'Parnassus' (1497) and Pontanus' "Urania"—read, Gombrich says, with this preface first then included, to Pontanus' Academy in 1501. See "An Interpretation of Mantegna's Parnassus", *Symbolic Images*, pp. 83-84 and nn. 10 and 11.

19 The famous academy at Naples was named after this Pontanus.

20 E.g., such a figure as of 'Theologia' in the 15C engraving (c. 1470) in the important series, 'Masters of the Tarocchi' (see App. III). Pat Rubin has drawn my attention to this figure (Plate 43, p. 123). 'Theology' has two faces: a young one and an old (this might suggest an etymological play: *novus* and *vetus* in L. doubling to mean young and old, as of persons; or New and Old, as of the two Testaments). What may interest us more, in the present context, is Theology's position in half-figure, posed behind and above a large starry sphere: i.e., she occupies the same situation as that of Raphael's 'Urania'. The 'Urania' figure in the Tarocchi series (Plate 24, p. 102), simply shows her as holding a (smaller) celestial globe in one hand and compasses in the other. The editors quote Tervarent: "The starry sphere which is [Theology's] attribute shows that she represents the study of things celestial". These two engravings illustrate the ease with which the study of the heavens or spheres (astronomy) becomes conflated or equated iconographically with the study of 'things celestial' (divine). For further early and also later emblems, see App. III.

21 It is evident that from the 15C onward until at least into the mid 17C, emblems themselves were recombining and conflating: as may be seen from the overlapping details in such figures as those of Astrology, Urania, Cosmography, Poesy and Theology, and in the progressive funnelling of many of the iconographical details, over the course of two centuries, into certain figures, notably those of 'Astrology' or 'Urania' (see, again, App. III). But in any case—where did the emblems themselves emanate from? From literary texts, of course! ("Tirées des anciens Autheurs"—J. Baudouin, *Iconologie*, pref., p. 1). Baudouin in the same preface stresses the close approximation between 'images' or paintings and poetry or oratory in both ancient and modern times.

22 The lyric poem of 71 lines was prefixed by Du Bartas to the 1579 edition of "L'Uranie", in *La Muse Chrestiene*: see U. T. Holmes *et al.*, Vol. II, pp. 73-74, prefatory note. Italics in the quotations are mine.

www.ingramcontent.com/pod-product-compliance
Lightning Source LLC
LaVergne TN
LVHW010629100826
845148LV00014B/3172

* 9 7 8 0 9 2 0 6 0 4 2 3 6 *